Weal with a Why

How to Invest, Give, and Live

for a Sustainable and Thriving Future

Presented by Practical Acts and Partners

Cazenove Capital
Charity 21
Environmental Funders Network
Ethex
Impact Investing Institute
Impact Shakers
Impatience Earth
Unburdened Solutions

Stuart Mills & Stephanie Mills

To Ben and Ryan,
your future is bright!

Dear Justin,
Thank you so much
for your support.
[illegible], Steph

Acknowledgement

This guide was something of an experiment in helping two ordinary people articulate their experience in the world of finance and philanthropy. Without the extraordinary people who helped us along the way, our story would be incomplete. Thank You!

Thank you to our collaborators: Thank you for seeing a spark in us and growing it into a flame together! Thank you for your unwavering encouragement to write our story and to strengthen our words with your expertise and enthusiasm. Thank you for your patience with our dodgy Zoom links and your keen eyes on the many iterations.

Yasmin Ahammad, Lisa Ashford, Jane Cabutti, Hannah Dillon, Julie Dunn, Sarah Farrell, Melissa Gilmour, George Harding-Rolls, Sarah Hughes, Alina Klarner, Rebecca Kowalski, Sophia Omar, Louisiana Salge, Emilie Shaw

Thank you to our 'project friends': We are so grateful for your helping hands, meaningful conversations, and brilliant insights we've had the deep privilege to share with you.

Alex Day, Justin Dekoszmovszky, Brian Dunhill, Paris Jordon, Nick Marple, Ergem Senyuva, Fancy Sinantha, Tim Stumpf, Antoinette Vermilye, John Vermilye, Alan Whittle

Thank you to our portfolio partners: Your dedication to making the world a better place inspires us every day. Equally, your willingness to help us better understand your work, allowing us to participate with you, has been a great privilege. Thank you for all that you do.

Ben Coles, Emma Crane, Simon Davis, Lynette Huntley, Lani Martin, Florence Miller, Philip Norman-Butler, Agamemnon Otero, Martin Petry, Cam Ross, Erica Wax

A special thanks to Versha Jones for bringing our message to life through your professional skill and personal passion for climate action. Thank you for your commitment to saving the planet!

About the Authors

Stephanie earned a post-graduate degree in not-for-profit management. Her career spans diverse roles from public relations to board leadership. She is dedicated to community empowerment, climate action, and social entrepreneurship, evidenced by her involvement with the Environmental Funders Network, Groundwork London's Our Space Awards, and Impact London Collective. Her love of nature started as a child, first shaped by the surrounding wide open expanse of the High Sierra Desert in Northern Nevada, and continues to grow now along the wild banks of the River Thames near her home in London.

Stuart is a senior executive focused on helping leaders navigate future uncertainty. As an innovator, intrapreneur, and changemaker, architecting complex, multi-million-pound transformations for global firms like Salesforce and Wood Mackenzie, he understands that the greatest risk in a disrupted world is not having a clear compass. His experience proves that while traditional playbooks are failing, a deep commitment to ethics provides the clarity and stability needed to make sound decisions amidst chaos. Today, through his work as an adviser and his engagement with the League of Intrapreneurs and the BMW Foundation Responsible Leaders Network, he helps leaders embed this ethical resilience into their operating models, building organisations that are not just profitable, but durable enough to thrive in the decades to come.

Table of Contents

Look Out for More

Given the complexity of all things financial and the wide breadth of topics, you will find content in different formats to help keep you moving down the path toward purposeful investing:

Explore More....

Resources, facts and figures that allow you to further deep dive into a topic.

Watch Out...

Warnings and tips for information that might give you pause.

Think about...

Ideas for you to consider and questions to answer at your own pace

Quick tips....

Look out for these little gems where we call out our best tips!

Did You Know?...

Interesting facts and figures

The views represented here are those of Stuart and Stephanie Mills. The guide resonates with their practice, but they recognise that your needs may differ and that there will be other resources available to you, specific to your interests, location, or needs. It aims to help you identify the types of services and financial vehicles to seek in order to meet your financial needs and values whilst serving the planet.

OUR WHY

We are worth more than our money. By harnessing our personal agency and leading through our actions, we choose a thriving life for all people and places.

INTRODUCTION

INTRODUCTION

The Narrators

We are Stephanie and Stuart Mills, an American-British couple with teenage sons who have called London home for the past two decades. As avid runners, we can often be found along the scenic routes of the Thames or Richmond Park. Our journey into the climate crisis is shaped by distinct backgrounds: Stuart began his career as an engineer in the Royal Navy before moving into the oil and gas industry, while Stephanie's professional life was initiated in land conservation.

We describe ourselves as **"Some Net Worth"** individuals, a term we have coined to describe circumstances in which we have built significant assets over the years, but with counterbalances. Although we are in the highest tax bracket, we don't have the liquidity that would make us fit the financial sector's definition of **High Net Worth** because we have more liabilities and variables in our mix. We are acutely aware of how shifting political and economic landscapes can profoundly impact our financial stability and future aspirations. In addition to our fortunate financial position, we also like to contribute to our community, and we feel a strong responsibility for caring for the planet. Here are some financial markers that make us see ourselves as 'some net worth' individuals:

- Two-parent household with a sole high-income earner
- Two children in secondary school (with an expectation that they will attend university)
- Homeowners with an interest-only mortgage
- Pension holders of multiple pensions from previous employers
- Shareholders of company stock through employee purchase plans and options
- Clients of a financial adviser
- Retail Bank Saving and Cash ISA account holders

We believe that those like us, of some net worth, possessing significant assets but often overlooked by traditional financial definitions, represent an under-recognised yet powerful source of capital for driving meaningful climate action. When we embarked on our learning journey, we quickly discovered that our money is not the only currency of "better" in our lives: be more connected to our communities, feel confident and proud of our actions, speak out against injustice, and participate in something bigger than ourselves. Our 'doing better' makes our lives more vibrant.

We offer you our story of how we reignited our love of land and sea when we asked ourselves, 'Can we do better with our money?', which spearheaded our deep dive into the world of sustainable finance.

The Partners

We are far from alone on this journey, and our story is one of many.

The guide that follows has been co-created with an abundance of collective intelligence and goodwill.

We found our expert partners through conferences, reports, serendipitous meetings, and bold conversations– all driven by a shared commitment to making intentional financial decisions more inviting, accessible, and rewarding.

While we are the guide's narrators, its richness comes from the hive mind. We encourage you to reach out, learn from our partners' work, and be part of this growing movement toward systemic change.

Cazenove Capital

Charity 21

Environmental Funders Network

Ethex

Impact Investing Institute

Impact Shakers

Impatience Earth

Unburdened Solutions

Our Learning Journey

Neither of us have a finance background. Stephanie's education and work experience are in public relations and charity management in the environmental sector, whilst Stuart's education and expertise are in business administration and change management. Over the years, our shared interest in 'good businesses' grew – especially as social entrepreneurship began to blur the lines between for-profit and nonprofit models.

We took a dive into our personal investments, taking stock of where our money was invested, and asking ourselves how we could actively align our money with our climate purpose. What we expected to be a guided tour with a financial adviser quickly became an adventure through an uncharted jungle – a maze of financial jargon, global goals[1], misleading media messages, and greenwashing financial services.

To navigate this jungle, Stephanie enrolled in a Sustainable Finance course at Cambridge University's Centre for Sustainable Leadership. It was a giant leap into the unknown, but she discovered a spectrum of financial activity to 'rewire the economy to a sustainable, inclusive economy[2].' Most importantly, she learned that

---

[1] United Nations. (n.d.). The 17 Goals. Sustainable Development Goals, Retrieved from https://sdgs.un.org/goals

[2] University of Cambridge Institute for Sustainability Leadership (CISL). (2017). Rewiring the Economy: Ten tasks, ten years. Retrieved from https://www.cisl.cam.ac.uk/resources/cisl-frameworks/rewiring-the-economy

an individual's capital can be influential – if deployed collectively, practically, and with intention.

This guide is our long answer to helping us find our way through the financial landscape with all of our capital. When we didn't find an immediate, single answer to our question of 'doing better with our money', we became curious about why there were no easy solutions. And, we quickly learned that our financial capital was only one part of the tools we had to offer. Our human capital (network and skills) would help us fully participate in climate action.

We are standing at
'climate crossroads'
in this decisive decade
for climate change.

PART 1

THE PURPOSEFUL INVESTOR

Your Agency and Climate Urgency

It's easy to feel like global challenges are just too big and complex for us as individuals to make a dent. But the truth is, we're not powerless.

We strongly believe in the **agency of individuals**. While governments, businesses, and financial institutions play significant roles, we cannot afford to wait for them. True change often begins in our everyday lives. We can create the future we want to see by using our roles as parents and grandparents, citizens and consumers, employees and employers, neighbours and investors. The more agency we feel in each of our roles, the more impact we can have.

At the end of 2020, like many people, we were trying to do something–anything–that connected us and helped us feel useful in the COVID-19 pandemic. The world seemed paradoxically more interconnected and more isolated at the same time. Many of the implications of Covid were becoming clearer: the widening gap between rich and poor, the erosion of women's rights, and racial inequality, to name just a few. Then there was the call for climate action, placing 2030 as the new 2050. The alarm bell rang. If we had any hope of saving our planet, it needed to happen now, not in 30 years' time, but in the next 9 years. So, what could we do?

We also believe in breaking down complex issues into achievable steps, where we can start taking action and witness tangible outcomes, at once empowering and motivating. Take climate change as an example. Instead of feeling paralysed by the enormity of the issue, we can focus on things we can control.

We engaged with the campaign Make My Money Matter, an awareness campaign that exposes how most pensions underpin the fossil fuel industry. Our retirement funds, which we wouldn't touch for another 20 years, would inevitably wreak far more environmental damage than our daily habits could ever offset. But there were alternative options, and we had the power to switch.

We read The Future We Choose by Christiana Figueres and Tom Rivett-Carnac. They posed two future scenarios: one darkly pessimistic and one of vibrancy and resilience. The choice was obvious! We also became weekly listeners to their podcast Outrage and Optimism, which brought the issues of climate change to life and solidified our resolve to act.

And, in 2020, the global economy was signalling change: a narrative from business and governments alike to Build Back Better, recognised that we had a rare opportunity to reboot the economy with greener, more just intentions. 2020 was a boom year for tech companies - the backbone of the new work-from-anywhere reality. For us personally, this meant Stuart's company's share value skyrocketed.

"Right," we said. "Let's do it!" But, what exactly was 'it'? We set ourselves a new challenge: to 'build back better' on a personal level, and make our money a tool for meaningful action.

Fast forward to today, and we know the world is very much in flux, and the climate crisis has intensified. It's important for us to remember that systemic change requires time and persistent effort, and we need to be patient with ourselves and others. Starting small and gradually increasing our involvement is perfectly acceptable. Don't wait for the perfect moment; every journey begins with a single step. By taking consistent action – however small it may seem – we build momentum, gain confidence, and inspire others to join the movement.

"I remember in 2020 when I first walked by a tree in our local park where someone wrapped a sign inviting others to create a rock garden. At its base was a small collection of painted stones, perhaps an afternoon's project to keep the children entertained for a few hours as I'd done on many such afternoons that Spring. Over the following days and weeks, more and more stones appeared, some saying thank you, some with names of loved ones lost. One tree was not enough, and the messages spread over several trees.

As I lay my stone down, I had a little moment of pride in the community coupled with gratitude for all the kind thoughts laid before me. I had a real sense of being part of something bigger, even as I stood next to the tree by myself. For me, this little rock garden brings home the simplicity of generosity in the messiness of life. Acts of kindness can both stand out as extraordinary or make up the fabric of our everyday: it's our choice in how we act and who we are."

- Stephanie

Your Capital And the Power of Generosity

Our first guiding principle is we believe that **each of us has much to offer beyond our wealth.** In fact, we do ourselves and the planet a disservice by ignoring the whole picture of who we are, what values we hold close, and what we offer that's unique to us as individuals.

We began with a simple realisation that understanding our values was crucial to making meaningful decisions about our finances and our lives. By recognising, and leaning into our core beliefs, we found clarity in our path forward. This process of self-discovery was invaluable, as it helped us understand that we had much to offer beyond just our financial resources.

As we aligned our actions with our values, we experienced a ripple effect that extended far beyond the initial act of giving. This alignment not only benefited others but also enriched our own lives in unexpected ways:

- Giving our time made us more invested in people and causes.
- Sharing our skills improved our expertise.

- Connecting friends with colleagues spurred greater results for all involved.

We also discovered a deep connection between generosity and nature: exposure to the natural world made us more trusting, helpful, and generous.[3] This beautiful benefit of nature only strengthened our resolve to protect our environment.

To discover our personal combination of values, we've used tools like Brene Brown's list of values and the GenAI tool TIGG. Narrowing the list down to 3 words that resonated with us was a powerful exercise. Reflecting on how we saw ourselves in each word, and how it made us feel, helped us apply these values to our actions with greater intention.

Try out Infectious Generosity's TIGG or Giving Tuesday's Generosity Toolkit to find actions that match your interests and values!

Stuart values Courage, Equality, Honesty, and Trust. Stephanie values Stewardship, Kindness, and Creativity. Together, we value Ingenuity, Community, Empathy, and Enthusiasm.

[3] Dose of Nature. (n.d.). A selection of studies demonstrating some of the benefits of exposure to nature. Retrieved from https://www.doseofnature.org.uk/studies1

All Your Capital

In economic terms, an individual's financial capital represents their money and assets, while their human capital embodies skills and knowledge, both of which are crucial for securing economic well-being and future opportunities. Beyond our financial resources, **we can all leverage our skills, time, stories, and networks** to build a sustainable and thriving future. We can dedicate our time to meaningful work as well as consciously direct our financial resources, unlocking our potential as agents of change.

Philanthropy Together describes human capital in a more, well, human way. They name an individual's capacity for giving of themselves in the 5 Ts: treasure, time, talent, ties, and testimony.[4]

And focusing on our "5 Ts" helped us identify how we could translate our values into actions:

Treasure: Making purposeful investments and donations, even small ones, to causes we care about.

Time: Volunteering or getting involved in community projects.

Talent: Sharing our skills and knowledge with those in need.

Ties: Using our networks to raise awareness and connect resources.

[4] The 5Ts is a concept introduced by Sarah Lomelin, CEO of Philanthropy Together in her TED Talk. Retrieved from https://philanthropytogether.org/ted

Testimony: Sharing our experiences to motivate others and foster a shared sense of purpose.

Aligning Our Finances with Our Values

As we've become more aware of our values, we've found ourselves making more confident financial decisions. This alignment created a natural framework for decision-making, helping us navigate complex financial choices with greater clarity and conviction.

The power of generosity is not just a concept, but a transformative force that has reshaped our lives and our understanding of the world. Chris Anderson, curator of TED, introduced the concept of "infectious generosity," arguing that acts of kindness and giving have the potential to create a positive cascade effect throughout society. For us, generosity isn't just about helping others; it also has a profound effect on us as givers. We've experienced the emotional rewards of giving firsthand, which can often surpass those of receiving. By giving, we've enriched our own lives, enhancing our sense of happiness and contentment through consciously and intentionally investing with our financial and human capital. By embracing generosity and aligning our actions with our values, we've created a more fulfilling life for ourselves and, we hope, a more positive impact on the world around us.

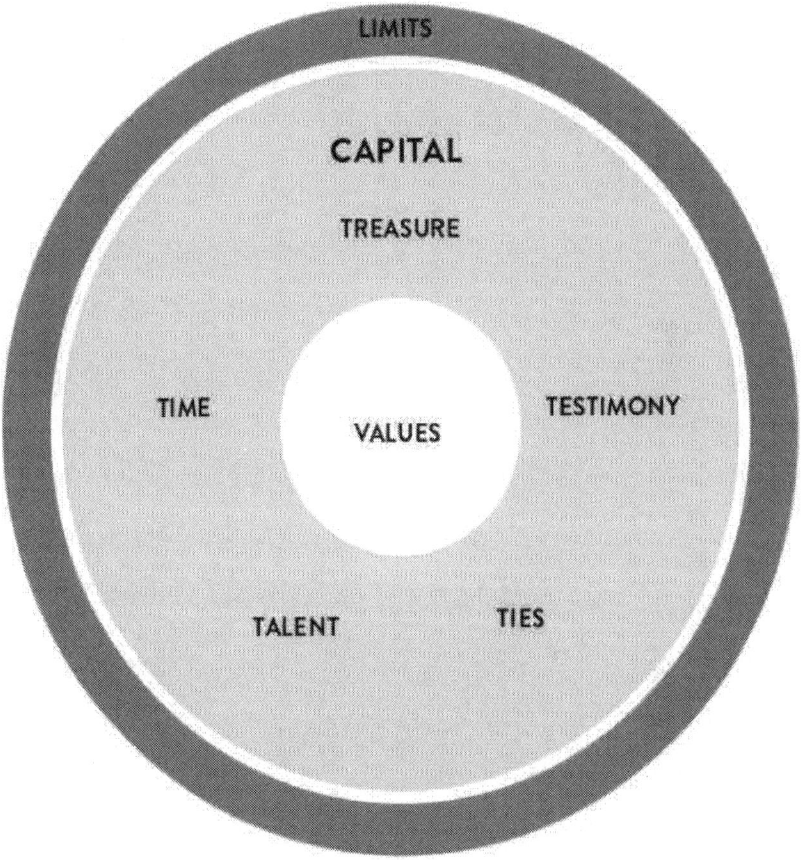

ALIGNING CAPITAL WITH VALUES

Remember, generosity doesn't require grand gestures or significant wealth. It's about finding ways to align with your current financial situation and values.

Mapping Your Capital to Impact

The **spectrum of capital** is a framework used by the financial services industry to demonstrate different ways in which money can be used for impact based on financial return. There are many different iterations of the spectrum of capital, but for our purposes, we simplified the range of options to 3 approaches. Finance first, impact investment, and philanthropic giving represent distinct approaches to deploying financial capital, each with a different primary focus and set of objectives. To define the three areas in the simplest terms:

- **Finance First** focuses primarily on financial returns, irrespective of impact.
- **Impact Driven** blends financial returns with measurable positive impact.
- **Philanthropic Giving** prioritises positive impact, without the expectation of financial return to the donor.

These three approaches work together to make up our overarching financial strategy. As we considered how our capital could contribute to a better world, we discovered opportunities across the entire spectrum. The more we embraced this strategy, the more we realised that diversifying gave us greater agency, allowing us to support the causes we care about while still meeting our desired level of risk and return.

Our journey with the spectrum of capital began with wanting to align our investments with our values. We started with what we had. We planned for our future, factoring in desired returns, and bolstered aims with positive impact.

It's not just about allocating capital to different asset classes, it's about a mindset shift: we realised that all capital—whether we recognise it or not—shapes the world in some way, either positively or negatively. Instead of passively allowing our capital to fuel impacts we were unaware of, we began to see it as a powerful tool for positive change—one that could help build a better world while also achieving our financial goals. So far, we've experienced these benefits from embracing a spectrum of capital approaches in both our investments and giving:

- **Expanded our impact**: By engaging across the spectrum, we've been able to support a wider range of causes and organisations that are making a difference in the world.
- **Deepened our understanding**: The spectrum has provided us with a framework for understanding the different ways that capital can be used to create positive change.

- **Increased our agency**: By actively managing our capital across the spectrum, we've gained more control over how our money is used and the impact it has.
- **Aligned our investments with our values**: The spectrum has helped us to ensure that our investments are consistent with our values and contribute to a better world.

You can choose to spread risk and also diversify your investments or pensions to those that favour positive social and environmental change. Understanding these different roles can help you decide which asset class works best for you and your aims, while the spectrum helps you to see the overall impact of your decisions. For example, choosing an investment account (traditional) is very different to donating to a cause, but each has a ripple effect toward collective action. While philanthropic giving may not be your sole focus due to a need for financial returns, it can still play a significant role in how you interact with the various forms of capital. When we see philanthropy as an investment on the spectrum of capital, its importance shifts from a 'nice to have' to a 'needs to happen' and can become an integral part of our investment strategy.

Taking stock of all your financial and human capital is a great way to ground yourself for your journey. At first, we looked at finances only, but now we plan ahead, including our time, skills, and connections. When we reviewed our actions over the course of the last few years, we surprised ourselves with how quickly our actions added up. Also, we saw decisions that were right for us at the time, but that now it was ok to change tack because 'our why' changed.

Think about your stage in life now. What, who, or where is important to you? Try to write down everything, no matter how small.

DID YOU KNOW?

Actions Help Drive Shifts to Demand

Public concern about plastic pollution, driven by thousands of ordinary people reducing plastic use and signing petitions, led to a major policy shift in 2015. By 2015, the collective actions—individuals choosing reusable bags and voicing demands—resulted in England introducing a 5p charge on single-use plastic bags, later increased to 10p, reducing usage by over 95% in major supermarkets.

Your engagement with financial institutions can drive where money is invested and demanding more sustainable investment options and stewardship, we can all push for a shift toward responsible investment. There's a growing expectation for financial institutions to not only report their financial performance but also to be transparent about their broader societal impacts and hold themselves accountable for delivering and increasing positive outcomes. This rising awareness presents a chance for each of us to align our investments with our values.

Your Worth And Power of the Collective

Our second guiding principle is the belief that **each of us is the greatest platform for change**. We all have different roles to play, offering the opportunity to engage ourselves in climate action every day.

As citizens, we have a voice in shaping government policies. Engaging in conversations with policymakers, advocating for change, and participating (e.g., voting) in the democratic process can contribute to a more just and equitable society. As well as engaging directly, we can fund organisations and campaigns that enable others to do the same.

As community members, we can participate in our neighbourhoods, whatever form that takes. For us, that means volunteering with the local Neighbourhood Watch scheme and helping our PTA at our sons' school. By lending our hands to one thing, we open up more conversations about other things that are important to us, like climate action or social justice.

As consumers, our purchasing decisions carry significant weight. By choosing to support companies that prioritise sustainability, ethical practices, and fair trade, we can create a powerful market signal. When we align our spending with our values, we encourage businesses to adopt more responsible practices.

And let's not forget one of our most powerful, and often overlooked, platforms: **our work**. Whether you're an employee, an entrepreneur, or a board member, your influence inside a workplace can be profound. You can advocate for more ethical sourcing, champion employee well-being, push for inclusive hiring, or steer your company's strategy toward sustainability. You can ask where your company banks, who it contracts with, and whether its pension options align with its values. You can ask it to offer payroll giving, and potentially to match what staff members give. If you run your own business, you have even more autonomy: you can build a culture that puts people and planet at the heart of profit. In short, your day job can be a daily act of alignment.

All these roles formed valuable parts of our philanthropy, using our private resources for the public good, equipping us with more agency than perhaps we first realised. Our relationships form the cornerstone of our actions, whether with our employer and colleagues, advisers and mentors, friends and family, or our broader community. The more we can develop ties to others and trust our people, the more powerful our actions become.

Power of the Collective

When policymakers, businesses, and financiers come together to collaborate around a common goal, they can significantly increase their collective impact. But when individuals come together, we amplify our impact and create a force that's difficult to ignore. Whether it's joining a local community group, supporting a cause through donations, or simply having conversations with friends and family about the issues we care about, our collective efforts create a powerful wave of change.

As the saying goes: 'If you want to go fast, go alone, if you want to go far, go together'. Collectives have been in practice in many parts of the world for a very long time, and these models are once again growing in popularity because people are finding the amazing personal benefits of doing more, together. People are coming together in all sorts of ways, pooling their '5Ts' and financial capital, to reach far more impactful results than they'd achieve on their own. Collective action is everything from a group of friends around a kitchen table who help a refugee family[5] to energy companies with cooperative ownership models.[6] Collective power is community: by participating in collective actions, we gain strength in our

---

[5] Dunn, E. (2019, April). *Helping others makes us happier – but it matters how we do it*. TED. Story retrieved from https://www.ted.com/talks/elizabeth_dunn_helping_others_makes_us_happier_but_it_matters_how_we_do_it

[6] Bristol Energy Cooperative is one example of a community benefit society. Retrieved from https://bristolenergy.coop/members/

convictions and build relationships with others in new, interesting ways.

No matter what form collective action takes, individuals connect and participate in a democratic, structured process, through collective pledges, to address an issue often too complex to be tackled alone. Members, whether through donation or ownership, have one vote regardless of the amount they contribute. The 'one member, one vote' rule allows for open participation of all who join. You might overlook or dismiss the simple act of voting. We found the act of voting to be a powerful motivator for us. We joined with our money, but by doing so, we committed to voting on actions of the organisation - thereby participating with our financial decision beyond the transaction alone.

What do collectives have in common?

- Shared Goals
- Members' participation
- Democratic decision-making: one member, one vote
- Pooling of resources
- A sense of community among members

The impactful careers charity 80000 Hours has a number of excellent articles and podcasts on safeguarding your mental health in impact-driven work.

Call to Action: Our World & Our Future

There is a growing consensus that our planet is in crisis, and that the interrelated impacts of climate change and nature loss have arrived. 2024 was the hottest year on record, with average global temperatures exceeding 1.5 degrees of warming above pre-Industrial levels for the first time – the threshold of global warming that the Paris Climate Agreement was designed to prevent. Unfortunately, based on current government-level climate commitments to 2030, global warming is currently on course to exceed 2.7 degrees.

Meanwhile, it was confirmed in 2023 that six of Earth's nine 'planetary boundaries'[7] – which include climate change, biodiversity loss, and land systems change – have now been crossed, meaning they can no longer function properly. Combined, this human-induced damage is disrupting the stability, resilience, and livability of the planet, causing record-breaking floods, storms,

[7] Planetary Boundaries are the highly interdependent systems and processes that create a safe operating limit for survival on Earth. Retrieved from https://www.ecomatcher.com/what-are-planetary-boundaries-and-why-are-they-significant/

heatwaves, drought, and wildfires – all of which are devastating the lives and livelihoods of countless communities around the world whilst crippling infrastructure and deepening food insecurity. The damages from inaction on climate change and nature loss are projected to rise to USD$38 trillion annually by 2050.[8]

Fortunately, continuation along this trajectory is not inevitable. Whilst we are the first generation to face this level of planetary crisis, we are also the first generation to have the global connectivity, knowledge, tools, and solutions available to address it. While public and private sector climate and environmental commitments cannot be relied upon to address these issues alone, we can and must step up to meet the moment. Everyone reading this guide has a vital role to play.

Solutions Are Ready Today

The good news is that a vast array of solutions is emerging to address these interrelated issues head-on, whilst building **community-based resilience** towards both the current and future impacts of climate change. Whilst the United States steps back on its climate and humanitarian commitments, others are stepping forward, whether at a country, state, city, island, or hyper-local level. Wherever we look, scalable and replicable solutions are being

[8] Potsdam Institute for Climate Impact Research (PIK). (n.d.). *Planetary Boundaries*

developed that can improve lives, drive economic growth, and tackle the climate crisis at the same time. Thanks to emotive, effective, and relentless campaigning, funding to support those most affected by climate change in the Global South is now projected to reach USD $300 billion annually by 2035, whilst low-carbon climate solutions such as Electric Vehicles and renewable energy are creating jobs, reducing bills, and improving health for millions of people worldwide.

We also have a collective responsibility to act. We cannot escape the fact that those least responsible for causing climate change are suffering most as a result of it, and that the 'quest for capitalism' - including uninhibited production and consumption - has made life significantly worse for the world's most vulnerable people, including through generating wealth that is actively (and successfully) being used to fund opposition towards climate action.

Envisioning a Future Worth Investing In

A better world is possible, and that starts with daring to imagine it. What does a thriving, just, and sustainable future look like to you? What are the values you want to see reflected in the world? For us, we like to imagine a world where the economy works for every human being, where everyone's potential is unlocked, and where Earth's systems cope with everyone without exceeding demands.[9]

This is about more than just daydreaming; it's about actively choosing to focus on the positive possibilities and then letting that vision guide our actions. We firmly believe that by making conscious choices with our time, talent, and treasure, we can shape a more just, sustainable, and prosperous world.

- **Invest in solutions, not problems**: We can shift our focus from what's wrong to what's possible. Instead of dwelling on the devastation of climate change, we can get excited about the multiple solutions that communities facing the impacts of climate change hold, as well as the potential of viable climate change solutions such as renewable energy and sustainable agriculture.
- **Amplify the good we see in the world**: We can all share stories of hope, resilience, and generosity. This helps counteract the negativity bias that can make the problems seem insurmountable.
- **Participate fully with all our capital**: We can show up for each other and find and support others, whether through our time, talent, testimony, or ties, to build the lives we envision.

---

[9] Doughnut Economics Action Lab. (n.d.). About Doughnut Economics. Retrieved from https://doughnuteconomics.org/about-doughnut-economics

When we start with a clear vision of the future we want to create, we're much more likely to find the motivation and energy to take meaningful action. We can't afford to wait for others to take the lead. The challenges we face demand immediate action. Our individual contributions, no matter how small, can collectively create a powerful force for positive change.

Impact investing
empowers you to
put your money where
your heart is.

PART 2

THE PURPOSEFUL INVESTMENT LANDSCAPE

Exploring the Landscape

The Spectrum of Capital[10] framework helped us visualise our allocations, but did not provide immediate answers as to how to allocate funds.

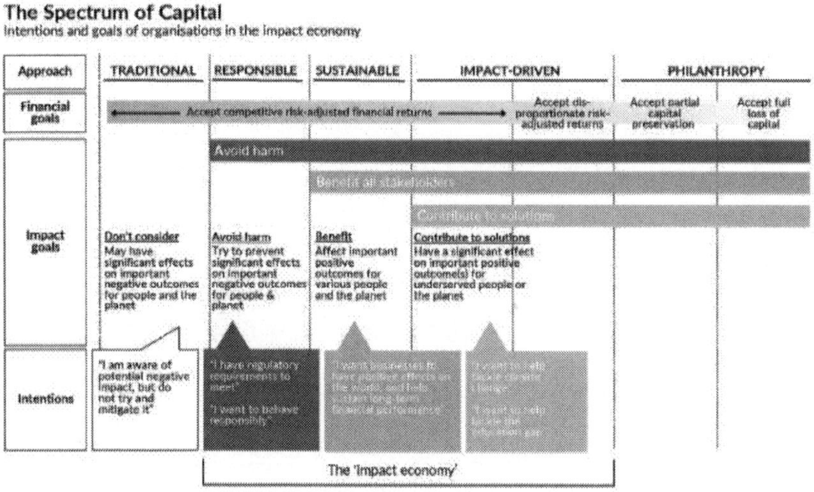

Source: The Rise Of Impact: Five Steps Towards An Inclusive And Sustainable Economy, UK National Advisory Board On Impact Investing, 2017 & Impact Management Project, 2017.

[10] The 'Spectrum of Capital' was first published in 2014 as part of the G8 Social Investment Taskforce. Retrieved from https://www.bvca.co.uk/our-industry/the-bvca-and-impact-investment/impact-investor-knowledge-hub/what-is-impact-investing.html

There was no one person, product, or service that would provide a portfolio working right across the spectrum at our level of net worth. Rather, we would require advice and information from many sources: all of whom use different terminologies, timelines, products, and approaches to the same end - putting our money to use for a 'better world', as we defined it.

Equally, we ran into daunting and difficult hurdles. However, more often than not, we found people very willing to help, even if they couldn't provide what we wanted. These conversations not only deepened our understanding of how our finances worked, but also how seemingly disparate issues are intertwined.

We explore the spectrum's three broad areas – traditional wealth management, impact investment and philanthropic giving – through a sustainable finance lens. The information introduces 'some net worth' investors to tools and services to consider when building a values-led portfolio; ways of engaging with these tools and services; and questions to ask across this spectrum.

To get started, we compare these areas of capital in the most simplest form:

Traditional Wealth Management

- **Primary Focus:** Generating financial returns and preserving capital for individuals, families, and institutions.

- **Objectives**: To grow wealth, manage risk, plan for financial goals (like retirement or education), and potentially transfer wealth to future generations.
- **Approach:** Involves analysing financial situations, setting financial goals, developing investment strategies (diversification across asset classes like stocks, bonds, and real estate), and ongoing monitoring and adjustments. The success is primarily measured by financial performance.

Impact Driven Investment

- **Primary Focus:** Generating positive, measurable social and environmental impact alongside a financial return.
- **Objectives:** To address pressing global challenges (e.g., climate change, poverty, inequality) while also achieving financial sustainability or profit.
- **Approach**: Involves intentionally investing in companies, organisations, and funds that aim to create specific positive impacts. This requires defining, measuring, and reporting on both financial and impact outcomes. Returns can range from below-market to market-rate.

Philanthropy

- **Primary Focus**: Contributing to the well-being of others and addressing societal problems through voluntary giving of our capital resources (not just our money).

- **Objectives:** To support charitable causes, promote social good, and create positive change in areas of social and environmental need, cohesion, or transformation.
- **Approach:** Typically involves making grants or donations to non-profit organisations or directly supporting charitable activities. The primary measure of success is the positive social or environmental outcome achieved, rather than financial return for the donor.

"I still remember the day when I was introduced to the 'spectrum of capital'. We had been on this purposeful wealth journey for a few years already and decided to support an education program with the Environmental Funders Network to help individuals and foundations understand impact investing. During one of the sessions the spectrum was introduced, almost in passing. Suddenly a lot of things fell into place and, like prams for new parents, I started seeing the spectrum of capital everywhere."

\- Stuart

‘Optimism is seeing challenges as opportunities to make progress.’

Hannah Ritchie,
Not the End of the World

Traditional Wealth Management

From our perspective as investors, we think about traditional wealth management as how we manage our money for long-term planning, as well as how we interact with various financial players, to invest using well-established routes. We engage with the following key services:

- **Our bank**: Not just for our everyday spending in our **current account,** but also through **savings accounts** and their **investment platforms,** as well as products such as **mortgages** and **credit cards**. While maybe not always the first thing we think of as 'wealth management', the money sitting in the bank is still part of our overall financial picture.
- **Our pension providers**: Whether it's a workplace pension or a Self-Invested Personal Pension (SIPP), these are key ways we're deploying capital for our future, and we often have choices about where the money is invested.
- **Our financial adviser** or **wealth manager**: A core part of traditional wealth management, they are the professionals we turn to for advice on how to best manage our wealth for the long term. They help us figure out our goals and risk tolerance. They traditionally recommend regulated investments.

What kinds of regulated investments are we talking about? Well, these are often publicly traded stocks or pooled funds where our money is combined with others and managed by professionals. Think of them like a big pot of money invested in various things. These come with some highly technical labels like Unit Investment Trusts or Open-ended Investment Companies (OEICs), but essentially, we recognise them as things like:

- Stocks of Individual Companies (Shares)
- Exchange-Traded Funds (ETFs)
- Mutual Funds

Often, we hold these investments within tax-advantaged products. These are like special wrappers that can help our money grow more efficiently by reducing the amount of tax we pay. The common ones are:

- Individual Savings Accounts (ISAs)
- Pensions
- Investment Bonds

Our wealth management is very much about us making active choices to engage with these various financial entities - banks, pension providers, financial advisers, and wealth managers - and utilising regulated investment vehicles, often within tax-efficient structures, to look after and grow our financial capital.

Be Curious About Values

Traditional wealth management, through engagement with your bank, pension provider, financial advisers, and wealth managers, can offer avenues to reflect your values. By actively engaging your advisers on their approach to responsibility, sustainability, and stakeholder considerations, and by seeking out funds with explicit environmental or social characteristics, you can steer your traditional investments in a more purposeful direction.

Engaging with the Wealth Management Industry

You'll often hear about **financial advisers**, **financial planners**, and **wealth managers**. While the terms can overlap and there's no strict definition, generally:

- A **wealth manager** often emphasises the **investment management** side of things, the actual 'looking after' of your investment portfolio.
- A **financial planner** tends to focus more on your overall **financial and life goals**, helping you create a plan to achieve them.
- A **financial adviser** is a more general term that can apply to both services.

For those with more significant wealth, larger wealth management firms might offer **managed services**. If your wealth is substantial, you might even get bespoke, tailored portfolios, depending on the manager's expertise.

To add to the confusion, wealth managers often refer to businesses or institutions that employ wealth managers, planners, and advisers. You may also come across **Independent Financial Advisers** who provide advice, planning, and management services. Whichever name they use, all these professionals are certified to provide "advice", a highly regulated activity overseen by the **Financial Conduct Authority (FCA)**.

ADVISERS AND THE PURPOSEFUL INVESTOR

Seeking financial advice from a trained professional, especially when you start adding impact to the wealth management aims, can prove invaluable. A wealth manager will be able to structure your wealth across the different vehicles to tailor it to your needs.

Using the well-established routes where most people start building wealth, advisers are well placed to help select appropriate investments based on the returns needed, the level of risk you are willing and able to take, and any ethical, social, and environmental outcomes that you wish to pursue.

The point of a wealth manager is to take ownership of structuring your wealth in line with your needs, or 'looking after' you and your investment for you. This "looking after" includes various services, but generally, these tend to be:

- Understanding your financial needs and how much risk you can handle when investing
- Choosing investments that will meet your needs while staying within the agreed risk limits
- Taking care of the paperwork and taxes that come with building, using, or protecting your wealth

Your wealth manager should, therefore, be able to give you advice on how to reflect your values and impact goals across your wealth. Note, however, it is not mandatory, and expertise in sustainable investing varies widely across the industry. Remember, it's your money, and you have the right to understand how it's being used and the impact it's having.

In recent years, the progress of sustainable finance has been frustrated by poor communication and loose use of language. The more people who talked about ESG and sustainable investing, the easier it became to be confused or to misunderstand what you were being told or indeed sold. Sometimes this can lead to 'greenwashing', making a fund or product appear sustainable without actually unders-tanding how it's sustainable.

The good news is that the Financial Conduct Authority (FCA) is seeking to tackle this problem with its evolving Sustainability Disclosure Requirements (SDR) regulation. Anti-green-washing rules were the first part of the SDR regulations to be introduced and are now fully embedded across all financial product providers. All claims to be green or environmentally and socially positive must be clear, fair, and not misleading.

A Green Look at How They Work

Traditional wealth management has historically focused primarily on maximising **financial returns**. However, it's increasingly common for Environmental, Social, and Governance (ESG) factors to be incorporated into investment decisions as a way to identify risks and opportunities that could impact those returns. This doesn't automatically mean harmful investments are excluded or more sustainable ones are favoured; it's more about understanding potential financial implications.

Keep in mind that the **Financial Conduct Authority (FCA)** regulates these activities to protect investors. They're also working on regulations like the **Sustainability Disclosure Requirements (SDR)** to bring more clarity to sustainable investing options, although these are still evolving.

FINANCIAL VEHICLES

When you're diving into traditional wealth management, you'll often come across a few key financial vehicles. These are the main ways your money is held and can grow:

- **Bank accounts:** These are your everyday spending and savings pots. It's worth noting that even in these seemingly simple accounts, the bank uses your deposits for things like loans, which can include financing for the fossil fuel industry.
- **Pensions:** These are your long-term retirement funds. You might have various pensions from different employers.

- **ISA/JISA/SIPPS:** These are tax-efficient savings and investment accounts. You can have a standard cash ISA, a Junior ISA (JISA) for children, or a Self-Invested Personal Pension (SIPP) for more control over your retirement investments.
- **Stocks:** These represent shares in publicly traded companies.
- **Bonds:** These are essentially loans you give to governments or companies, which they repay with interest. This includes government bonds like UK gilts.
- **Funds:** These are pooled investments where your money is combined with others to invest in a range of assets like stocks and bonds. A professional investment manager makes the decisions about what to invest in.**Investment portfolios:** Banks or investment platforms can help you create a mix of these assets tailored to your needs and risk tolerance.

DID YOU KNOW?

Big Banks

Banks have financed $6.9 trillion to fossil fuels since 2016

(Rainforest Action Network, 2023)

Bank Accounts

Your day-to-day spending from your credit card or current account is delivered by who you choose to bank with. Banks play a pivotal role in the world as a primary funder of loans and credit facilities. Your bank may use the money you deposit with them to offset their loan book. These loans can be to a range of different companies, including the likes of fossil fuel producers.

So, while these are your short-term spending pots, who you choose to bank with can have an impact on the world, based on your bank's lending activities. Asking your bank about their **net-zero commitments** and fossil fuel financing policies can help you understand if their climate ambitions align with your own.

Here are some attributes you could look for in a bank to ascertain its climate ambitions:

- Is the bank a member of the Net-Zero Banking Alliance?
- Have they made a net-zero commitment?
- Do they have emission reduction commitments that cover scope 1, 2, and 3, including financing activities?
- Do they have a commitment to end or phase down fossil fuel financing, particularly for fossil fuel expansion activities (creation of new streams of oil, gas, or coal)?
- Are emissions reduction targets based on absolute emissions or intensity of emissions? The latter allows for an increase in absolute emissions so long as low-emission activities increase proportionately.

DID YOU KNOW?

British Public Want to Invest Sustainably

Multiple surveys suggest that a majority of the British public wants to invest sustainably. The Financial Conduct Authority's (FCA) Financial Lives survey of 2022 indicated that 81% of those asked wanted their money to do some environmental and social good, as well as generate a financial return. Unfortunately, the number of people who are currently investing sustainably is disproportionately lower than this.

Many advisers do not have permission from the regulator (or appropriate insurance cover) to give advice on individual company stocks and shares, crowd-funding, peer-to-peer lending, or illiquid investments (i.e., property).

So, when we wanted to fund a local community energy project, for example, our adviser was unable to help, not because they weren't interested, but because they may not have had the necessary regulatory permissions and expertise in advising across the full investment spectrum.

Pensions

Analysis from Make My Money Matter (MMMM), Aviva, and Route2 suggests that making your pension green is more powerful at cutting your carbon footprint than giving up flying, going veggie, and switching energy providers.[11] This staggering estimate reflects the fact that how your pension is invested defines what your long-term capital is funding.

We can all be asking our employers where our pension is invested and pushing for green solutions. Make My Money Matter has ranked the 12 largest UK pension providers on their climate plans. If you're not happy with how yours scores, contact your employer to highlight their climate performance and demand action for a greener pension Climate Action Report - Make My Money Matter.

ISA/JISA/SIPPS and Investment Portfolios

Your bank may offer investment portfolios, or you may utilise an investment platform to choose your own long-term investments. Unless you have the expertise to choose individual companies to invest in, most self-selectors will choose a pooled fund. This is

[11] Pension Bee. (2025, January). Three reasons to think about where your pension is invested. Pension Bee Blog. Retrieved from https://www.pensionbee.com/uk/blog/2025/january/three-reasons-to-think-about-where-your-pension-is-invested

where a professional investment manager chooses the underlying investments in line with the objective of the fund. For instance, a global equity fund may look to invest in circa 50 companies that the manager has identified that they believe will deliver strong share price returns.

Pooled Funds

Pooled funds allow a number of investors to allocate to the same strategy, thus creating economies of scale, aiding diversification, and allowing you the comfort that a professional is taking care of the underlying selection.

In the UK, funds that market themselves as Sustainable need to apply for a Financial Conduct Authority's (FCA) sustainability label. These funds must have clear sustainability objectives, with at least 70% of their investments supporting that objective and no holdings contradicting it. You'll find details in the fund's prospectus and a short Consumer Facing Document (CFD).

In Europe, funds are categorised under Article 6 (no sustainability scope), Article 8 (promoting environmental or social characteristics - often called 'light green'), and Article 9 (having sustainable investment as their objective - often called 'dark green'). Opting for article 8 or 9 funds can ensure a minimum standard of sustainability, with article 9 being the most ambitious.

FUND SUSTAINABILITY LABELS

UK Fund FCA Labels

(refers to those that are registered in the UK, rather than funds that exclusively invest in UK assets)

Sustainability Focus

FOCUS funds investing in assets that are environmentally and/or socially sustainable

Sustainability Improvers

IMPROVERS funds investing in assets that have the potential to improve their environmental and/or social sustainability over time

Sustainability Impact

IMPACT funds that aim to achieve a positive, measurable impact in relation to an environmental and/or social outcome

Sustainability Mixed Goals

MIXED GOALS funds investing in a combination of the other labels

European-registered Fund Labels

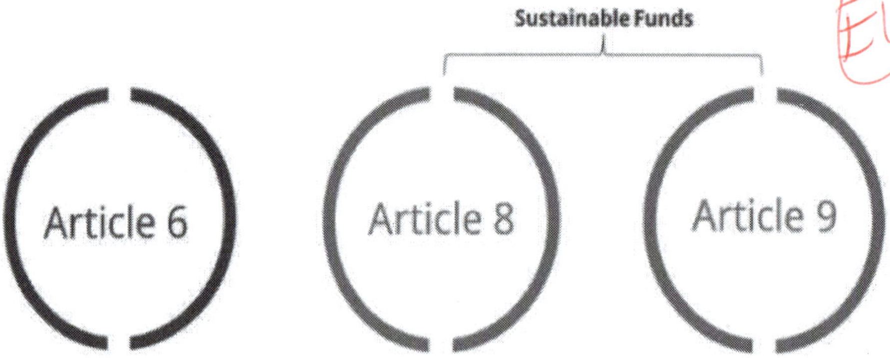

Funds without a sustainability scope

Funds that promote environmental or social characteristics (light green)

Funds that have sustainable investment as their objective (dark green)

You'll find details in the fund's prospectus and a short Consumer Facing Document (CFD), a succinct 2-page summary of the approach. This can help you identify what funds align with your own impact goals, and get a clear understanding of the outcomes each strategy is intending to achieve.

Be wary of being sold ESG integration as a means to improve the sustainability of your portfolio. It is a means to identify risks rather than avoid harmful sectors.

INVESTMENT STRATEGIES FOR PURPOSEFUL INVESTORS

Strategies in traditional wealth management usually focus on planning through risk, return, and tax efficiency, and with a green or ethical lens applied to your investments, you can add a fourth aim of sustainability to your values-led portfolio. Broadly speaking, this aim is measured by excluding negative investments or finding positive investments:

Screening Out

- **Exclusions** can be applied to investments involved in industries that create negative social and environmental impacts, such as tobacco producers and fossil fuel extractors. Model portfolios and sustainable funds often include a comprehensive list of exclusions based on revenue tolerances, typically capturing the main 'sin sectors', i.e., tobacco, gambling, pornography, alcohol, arms, fossil fuels, and predatory lenders. A wealth manager should be able to provide a detailed description of the excluded activities.

- **Tailoring exclusions:** Asking for more specific exclusions in model portfolios or funds, such as animal testing or fish farming, can be more difficult. However, your manager may be able to offer tailored portfolios that incorporate more specific exclusions. These will typically be directly invested (where the manager chooses the individual companies to invest in) rather than in pooled funds.

Check if the exclusions are applied on a direct-only basis (on any companies purchased directly in the portfolio) or a direct and indirect basis (where investments in any pooled funds would also need to adhere to the exclusion). Stating direct-only enables your manager discretion to buy any kind of pooled vehicle, which may have material underlying exposure to the types of companies you wish to avoid.

Specifying sectors where you won't invest does not mean that the rest of the portfolio would necessarily meet your sustainability expectations. You can exclude some activities and still own companies with very questionable practices and severe human rights violations to their name. Asking for a minimum ESG/Sustainability standard can help avoid such companies.

Positive Focus

A sustainable portfolio not only avoids harmful investments but seeks out those with strong sustainability characteristics: going beyond avoiding the bad towards actively doing good. For example, they may have exceptional employment practices that promote the well-being of their staff, or leading environmental policies that are helping the company transition to net zero. The portfolio should offer some form of sustainability reporting, which brings to life the sustainability characteristics.

ESG Integration

Involves the incorporation of ESG factors (qualitative or quantitative information) into investment selection. It involves understanding any material ESG weaknesses or opportunities of a business as a means to find better long-term investments. It does not necessarily mean excluding investments with poor ESG characteristics if the manager believes the financial opportunity outweighs the risk. ESG integration is almost standard practice across the investment industry.

Don't be afraid to say 'No!' to the nasties. Think Long Term! Even though exclusions might make our yearly returns jump around a bit compared to normal benchmarks, we expect things to even out over time.

EXPLORE MORE

What's the difference between ESG, Sustainable, and Responsible funds?

The terms ESG, Sustainable, and Responsible funds are often used interchangeably, as they share significant overlap in their focus on non-financial factors in investment. In practice, the lines can be blurry, and many funds will incorporate elements of all three approaches.

A simplified look at the terms:

ESG

Analysing risks and opportunities related to environmental, social, and governance factors to inform investment decisions (can be a tool within sustainable and responsible investing).

Sustainable

Investing with the aim of contributing to long-term environmental and/or social well-being alongside financial returns.

Responsible

Investing in a way that aligns with ethical and societal values, often involving exclusions and engagement, and can include both ESG and sustainability considerations.

Thematic Investing

Involves constructing a portfolio of assets that benefit from specific medium to long-term trends, f energy transition. Thematic funds focused on long-term structural environmental and social trends are commonly incorporated in sustainable strategies.

Your wealth manager should be able to offer you a sustainable portfolio. Know that different managers have different interpretations of sustainability, so ask your manager to explain what they mean by sustainable.

You can ask your wealth manager for sustainability reports that show what your investments are really doing. For example:

What's *their carbon footprint compared to others?*

How *many companies they invest in have plans to reach net zero?*

What's *the overall temperature rise expected if all investments were like theirs?*

These numbers come from different tools, so it's worth asking how they got them and what they actually mean in plain language.

engthening Strategy Through Stewardship

No matter which financial vehicles you deploy, your engagement with your financial services can make a big impact. This is where your human capital comes into your investment strategy:

- Take the time to engage with your bank, pension provider, employer, and financial advisers to learn more about their sustainability practices and your choices.
- Use your voice to ask for better choices.
- Vote! Shareholders have a commanding tool for creating change at their disposal when participating in Annual Shareholder Meetings.
- Tell others what you discover: both good and bad actions of companies can be highlighted on social media.

These are actions everyone can do, regardless of the amount of money in their pockets.

BUILDING RELATIONSHIPS

While the impact you can have with your investments is important, there is also an impact to be found in the influence you have with your adviser. You may find that the knowledge, encouragement, enthusiasm, and ideas that you bring to the table are passed on, like pollen between flowers, to other workers and clients of the firm.

At present, there is negligible coverage in the core "how to be a financial adviser" curriculum of how to manage your money sustainably or for positive impact. Most advisers will not have deep expertise in climate change, nature depletion, and social issues, nor the various ways in which capital might be applied to tackle these. There is, however, a wealth of educational material freely available both within the advice profession and externally, and advisers are expected to carry out a minimum of 35 hours of continued professional development each year. Some parties are petitioning for this to include a compulsory allocation to environmental and social issues and solutions, but until that becomes reality, you may wish to ask your adviser what learning they have undertaken in this area, or even request that they go and read or watch something.

What advisers are duty-bound to do, however, is carefully research the products and solutions that they offer. They also need to be transparent and clear about the opportunities and limitations that these may have in delivering on your financial goals, your values, and any specific impact you want to aim for.

DID YOU KNOW?

Barriers

There is real opportunity for growth in responsible investment approaches.

Of the £10 trillion managed by UK investment managers, £89bn is in responsible investment funds. That's less than 1% being managed in responsible investment approaches. That's a BIG GAP! Schroders' global investor survey suggests three main barriers to overcoming the gap:

PERFORMANCE:
concerns that sustainable investments will generate lower returns.

TRUST:
lack of transparency and fear of greenwashing.

ADVICE:
69% of people with a financial adviser have been given a choice to invest sustainably.

Source: IMA Investment Management Survey 21-22
Investment Management Survey 2021-22. full report.pdf (theia.org)

Don't be afraid to challenge jargon and demand clear, understandable answers!

The finance industry is notorious for its anachronisms and product complexities, so it's easy to be intimidated by jargon or numbers and feel a bit lost at times.

Advisers seek to have a long-term relationship with their clients, one where they can deliver trusted services that are needed and valued, enabling clients (and their children) to stay with them or recommend their services to others. Likewise, clients build relationships with their advisers over many years, trusting their expertise and sharing life's big milestones like starting a family, buying a home, reaching retirement, or planning inheritance.

It can therefore be helpful to be clear about the non-tangible aspects of your adviser's services that you value beyond the conventional practice:

1. **Helping you understand their products and services**, and how these can support your goals.

2. **Respecting and supporting your overall views and plans for impact**, even those that they can't directly assist with.
3. **Providing a range of investment options** and proof of thorough research into both the recommended products and the companies that offer them, and why they fit your needs.
4. **Using language that is easy to understand** and promotes productive conversations.
5. **Being open to exploring new ways of using capital** that align with ethical considerations and create positive change, even if it's different from their usual approach.

The climate crisis requires a shift in how financial advisers engage with clients, aligning investments with individual aspirations for a sustainable future. This is a substantial challenge, and the gap between a resilient future for us all and current financial advice practices is significant. To achieve better outcomes for the crisis we face, investors can actively steer their advisers towards responsible and impactful investment strategies. You can start a meaningful dialogue with your adviser and ensure that your financial strategy aligns with your desire for a more purposeful and sustainable future by focusing on your values and the impact you seek through your investments.

"The most impactful part of our strategy has been to apply a traffic light system across our entire portfolio. Like many portfolios, ours was based mostly on our risk profile and life commitments (think mortgage and school fees). We wanted to assess our holdings against a returns plus values benchmark, so we developed a 'traffic light system' to evaluate our holdings: green for aligned, amber for uncertain, red for problematic. The results gave us a clear map of what actions we could take."

- Stuart

‘Never doubt that a small group of thoughtful, committed citizens can change the world; indeed, it’s the only thing that ever has.’

Margaret Mead

Impact Investment

"Impact investing" was a new term to us, and one we didn't fully know how to approach when we first encountered the spectrum of capital. We soon learned that it's a rapidly growing area of financial services where we can closely participate in our investments. It allows us to make deliberate choices to manage our wealth by investing in things - companies, projects, or funds - with the clear intention to generate positive, measurable returns, for both social and environmental impact, plus financial gains.

While there can be a lot to consider in impact investments, we now know it's about us saying, "Right, my money can do more than just grow; it can actively help tackle some of the big challenges we face, like climate change or social inequality." Unlike traditional investing, where the primary focus is often solely on financial returns, with impact investing, we're deliberately seeking opportunities where our capital can create tangible good in the world while still aiming for some form of financial gain.

Our impact investments represent a small portion of our overall assets, but as we gain confidence in our strategy and choices available to us, we are able to invest more in these direct investments.

The degree of social or environmental impact can vary, of course. Investing in shares of a company on the stock exchange (even if it's a sustainable company) might have a lower direct impact than directly funding a new community wind farm, for example. But both can play a role in a purposeful portfolio.

Vehicles & Strategies in Impact Investment

While a large portion of UK impact investing is carried out by institutional investors (hedge funds, private foundations, banks, pension funds, and other fund managers), there are well-established web-based investment platforms that offer individuals an opportunity to invest directly in products that benefit organisations, creating positive impacts.

The main products offered by these platforms offer an alternative way to invest directly to align your money with your values, differing from that of traditional wealth management. Some typical vehicles in impact investment that you may come across include:

- Community Shares
- Ethical Bonds

- Innovative Finance ISAs (IF ISAs)
- Equity Investments in Impact-Focused Companies

Broadly speaking, common traits among impact investment vehicles are that they tend to have longer terms, higher risk, and variable liquidity. Whether you're funding a local community project, lending to ethical businesses, or investing in sustainability-focused companies, these options provide the opportunity to make a difference while potentially earning decent financial returns.

Community Shares

Community shares are a way for impactful community organisations, businesses, and cooperatives to raise flexible and affordable finance from individual investors to help them develop and grow. They are also known as withdrawable shares in a cooperative or community benefit society (CBS). Community shares are a way to invest directly in local projects that matter and enable individuals to support enterprises that make a real difference within communities.

Unlike shares in a publicly-traded company, community shares are withdrawable shares that cannot be sold, traded, or transferred between members. With a community share offer, supporters such as local residents and stakeholders become members of the business or organisation they invest in.

Ethical Bonds

Ethical bonds are a way to provide funding to organisations that are committed to making a positive social or environmental impact. Similar to other bond products, ethical bonds are issued by social enterprises or profit-for-purpose businesses to raise funds for fixed terms at a fixed interest rate, and the capital is repaid at the end of the term. These bonds are often used in large-scale sectors such as clean energy generation or sustainable transport. Unlike with community share offers, investors in bonds act as lenders and don't receive membership or voting rights.

Innovative Finance ISA (IF ISA)

An IF ISA is a tax-free investment alternative finance option, like peer-to-peer lending, often supporting businesses or **social enterprises** with an ethical mission. It lets you invest with the aim of growing your money tax-free while helping to make a positive impact on society and the environment. Returns depend on the success of the individual projects or businesses in the ISA, but your investment is directly tied to initiatives that are actively helping to combat climate change, reduce poverty, or build stronger communities.

Equity Investments in Impact-Focused Companies

Equity investments involve buying shares in businesses that have a mission to create a positive social or environmental impact. Investors then have an ownership stake in the business and the potential for financial growth. Some equity investments qualify for the **Enterprise Investment Scheme (EIS)** or **Seed Enterprise Investment Scheme (SEIS)** tax relief, which can provide significant tax advantages.

Unlike their financial cousin, the cash ISA, IF ISAs don't have FSCS protection, meaning funds are at risk if the business or organisation fails. These IF ISAs therefore carry higher risks than traditional ISAs due to the potential for default.

Engaging with Impact Investing

Impact Investing is about moving beyond ethical and sustainable finance decisions towards those that intentionally embrace social and environmental transformation, actively making investments that contribute to solutions. The important thing about this approach is that a real-world positive impact that also delivers financial returns is very possible.

WHAT IS DRIVING THE GROWTH OF IMPACT INVESTING?

The first driver is simple in some ways. Climate change, social inequality, and biodiversity loss have created urgent needs that traditional funding sources can't address alone. This represents a huge opportunity, which leads to the second driver, **client demand**: as the "Great Wealth Transfer" unfolds—with approximately £5.5 trillion transferring between generations in the UK over the next 30 years—younger investors are increasingly aligning their investments with their values, and firms are seeing this opportunity to tap into changing and growing client demand, offering products and services suitable for many different types of investors.

And thirdly is thanks to the government's response to these changes: Regulators and policymakers are looking to address the UK Financial Conduct Authority's Sustainability Disclosure Requirements regime, which includes impact-focused labels for retail investments, has brought greater clarity and credibility to the market. The new regime was set up to counteract some of the fears around *impact washing* and ***green washing,*** or in simpler terms, ensuring that investment products actually do what they say on the tin.

Check out this master list of resources by Aunnie Patton Power on impact investing (updated end of 2023).

ROLE OF DIRECT IMPACT INVESTING IN BALANCED PORTFOLIO

As the word 'direct' implies, direct impact investing cuts out the middleman. Direct impact investments can be considered part of a balanced, purposeful investment strategy, alongside investing in public equities or funds with an ethical or green focus, or working with a wealth manager or adviser, as discussed previously. It offers several benefits:

- **Tangible impact:** Direct investments allow you to see what your money is helping to achieve. You can often track the progress of the project you've supported, whether it's the number of homes powered by renewable energy or the number of jobs created in a disadvantaged community. This real-life connection gives these investments a stronger sense of purpose and reinforces the impact of your investment.
- **Diversification:** Direct impact investing can improve your investment portfolio diversification. It can give you the opportunity to invest in sectors and geographies that larger funds might overlook, potentially lowering overall risk and giving you exposure to innovative grassroots solutions.
- **Alignment with values:** You can choose projects that align with your personal values, whether it's taking positive climate

action, promoting financial inclusion, or supporting local communities.

- **Investing small as part of something big:** Direct impact investing services can offer opportunities to invest relatively small amounts (some investments start at just £50), making it more accessible to a wider audience. This creates a sense of an investor community, where many people contribute to achieve a shared goal. Even small investments can collectively make a big difference, empowering individuals to become active participants in creating positive change. This "small as part of something big" mentality is at the heart of direct impact investing.

Web-based Investment Platforms

Platforms aim to connect investors directly with enterprises working at a grassroots level to address some of our most pressing social and environmental challenges. They have seen firsthand how community-driven energy projects, social enterprises, and ethical businesses can thrive when backed by investors who refuse to accept that progress must slow down. The investment opportunities can range from community renewable energy projects and social enterprises to profit-for-purpose businesses and sustainable agriculture initiatives.

Angel Investments

Another option to align your money with your values is to invest directly in impact startups as an **angel investor**. Angel investments make up 50% of visible funding for early-stage companies in Europe[12]. By putting even small amounts of money towards validating and scaling environmental and/or social solutions at the very early stages, angel investors have a significant say in which solutions get off the ground.

Traditionally, angel investing has been reserved for only the most affluent, but innovations and government support have now made direct early-stage investing more accessible and attractive for a much broader part of the population, including:

- The emergence of **crowdfunding** and direct investment platforms that allow investors to invest from as little as £10.
- The emergence of **angel syndicates** accepting investment tickets from as low as £2,000, whilst also providing the opportunity to invest as part of a syndicate of investors and benefit from shared expertise during and after the investment.
- The introduction of **EIS and SEIS tax relief schemes** for the earliest investments, allowing investors to offset up to 50% of their investment amount, as well as any losses against their income tax or capital gains tax.

---

[12] European Business Angels Network. Angel Invetment Market Highlights 2023. Retrieved from https://www.eban.org/eban-annual-statistics-compendium-for-2023/

Direct impact investing can offer investors a powerful way to align their money with their values and play a vital part in building a more sustainable future. By connecting individuals directly with impactful projects, impact investment is helping to democratise finance and empowering everyone to use their money as a force for good, and innovative offerings for direct angel investments further expand possibilities for value-aligned direct investments.

It's important to remember that all investments carry risk, and you should always conduct your own research before making any investment decisions. However, direct impact investing gives you the potential for both financial returns and meaningful social and environmental impact, making it an important consideration within a balanced impact investing portfolio.

Join the Club!

Investor Clubs (often called Syndicates) are a great way to get started in impact investing because you can learn about issues and opportunities with other like-minded, interested individuals. Depending on the club, members can help be involved throughout the process from nomination, due diligence, selection, and then active participation in the company. Membership fees apply, and there may be a minimum investment, so look for clubs that are a good fit for your aims.

Intentionality

Impact investing is rooted in the premise of creating positive change alongside returns, but good intentions alone aren't always enough. Intentionality goes further, providing a framework for ensuring impact is not only pursued but also measured and accountable.

Intentionality comes into play when impact investing is central to how you manage your wealth. The Impact Investing Institute defines intentionality for investors as "an impact investor's deliberate goal is to contribute to specific positive and measurable social or environmental outcomes."

Intentions alone may not be enough to ensure your goals are met. That's where intentionality can be a useful practice. It helps you move from passive impact investing to a more accountable process for you and your fund managers.

So, what are some ways for you to practice intentionality?

- Always lead with your **values** and ensure they are communicated and understood.
- Be clear about your impact **goals** before choosing investments - be ready to convey them confidently.
- Actively seek sector or domain **expertise** - over time, you may also develop some of your own.

- **Leverage** your own professional experience, especially if it aligns with your impact goals - use those transferable skills to enhance your investment strategy and to evaluate its outcomes.
- **Question** expertise by asking curious or discerning questions, and don't be afraid to ask questions like "is the impact verifiable?", and if so, "how is this impact being measured?"
- Be **receptive** to talking about and understanding any negative impacts or trade-offs. Factor those into your investments and look for/discuss ways to mitigate them or pivot away.
- Stay **engaged** after the investment. Think about other ways you can help, like sharing industry contacts or offering extra resources.
- Consider **externalities** (or any factors) that may affect your impact goals, not just negatively but also positively, and be ready to course correct.

Leading voices in impact investing emphasise that intentionality involves both clarity and commitment. Without this, impact investment can unwittingly become virtue-signalling (known as impact washing). The best way to avoid this is to approach your impact investments as a true partnership where you continuously shape and assess outcomes in order to refine and improve your approach. However, always remember that progress matters far more than perfection.

When considering impact investing, think about these three things first:

1. **Look Beyond Returns Trade-offs**: "There is a consensus amongst our interviewees and survey respondents that impact investing can achieve market-competitive returns without sacrificing impact goals, and vice-versa," notes the Impact Investing Institute report.
2. **Consider the Full Spectrum**: Explore multiple asset classes, from private equity to public markets, to diversify your impact portfolio.
3. **Embrace Measurement**: While comparing impact results remains challenging, the ability to verify impact outcomes is improving, with 55% of investors reporting significant progress in this area over the past five years.

There are also several impact investing "influencers" who are very active on LinkedIn. It may be worth following these individuals for their regular insights and updates on the market and trends: Jamie Broderick, Harry Davies, and Aunnie Patton Power.

EXPLORE MORE

What is the Investment Risk Warning?

Each investment type comes with unique risks and rewards, so it's important to consider your goals and risk tolerance before diving in. When entering an investment site, especially when looking at impact-driven opportunities, you are likely to see risk warnings such as the following:

'Don't invest unless you're prepared to lose all the money you invest. This is a high-risk investment, and you are unlikely to be protected if something goes wrong. Take 2 mins to learn more.

or

'This communication is only intended for Investment Professionals, Professional Investors, Certified High Net Worth and Self-Certified Sophisticated Investors.'

The warnings are mandated by the Financial Conduct Authority (FCA), an independent financial regulator under the purview of the Treasury and Parliament. Its aim is to ensure fair markets by protecting individual consumers, the financial markets, and competition in the markets.

So let's take a closer look at what the FCA tells consumers about high-risk investments. There are five key risks identified in a '2-min read' for consumers to acknowledge when investing (See Ethex's sample).

1. You could lose all the money you invest

2. You won't get your money back quickly

3. Don't put all your eggs in one basket

4. The value of your investment may reduce

5. You are unlikely to be protected if something goes wrong

With these in mind, ask yourself 5 Key Questions to see if you are ready and willing to invest in these types of investments. The FCA provides good resources for evaluating your understanding of risk and preparedness for investments, especially new and different investment types.

We first found these warnings intimidating, making us stop our decision and question whether we could make the investment. But we now understand our own threshold for risk and reward, as well as the reason why the warning is in place.

‘Be brave. Give what you can, and then be absolutely amazed at what happens next.’

Chris Anderson,
Infectious Generosity

Philanthropic Giving

While we've highlighted how philanthropy is more than our purses, the financial aspect of our philanthropy gives us a powerful lever with which we can support social change. It's about using our financial resources to support initiatives that might not be ready for, or even suitable for, traditional investment models that expect a profit in return.

We think of philanthropic giving as our way to provide vital capital - the kind of funding that gets crucial projects off the ground, tests out innovative solutions, or challenges existing systems. This is where we focus on those deep-rooted social and environmental issues, supporting the organisations and efforts that are working to address the root causes and not just the symptoms.

Given the scale and complexity of the environmental challenges we are facing, people often ask: "What difference will my funding make?" In fact, philanthropic giving is exactly the kind of funding needed. Because it is society's most flexible capital, it can be deployed quickly, take risks, start movements, and test out solutions that other finance can then scale. Most powerfully, unlike other forms of finance, it can be used to challenge businesses and governments to do more, and to hold them to account to ensure they meet their promises and commitments. It's arguably the most catalytic form of finance in the face of social and environmental challenges, and the sort of funding most urgently needed.

Behind the scenes, philanthropic funding has been integral to almost every aspect of environmental action that has succeeded to date, from campaigns that lead to policy change such as the developments in ocean protection, or the launch and growth of accountability platforms such as CDP that encourage tangible corporate climate commitments, to powerful media and documentaries that increase the public's awareness (remember An Inconvenient Truth? This was co-funded by philanthropist Jeffrey Skoll). Philanthropy has helped get projects off the ground that would not have been possible without it.

Philanthropy can take a variety of forms, from long-term giving to one-off donations, all of which centre around the concept of using capital to generate positive social and environmental change. At its best, philanthropy can be a generous, progressive, and transformational way to address the systemic issues that perpetuate inequality and injustice around the world and make it a better, more equitable, and healthy place to live.

For inspiration, explore fantastic examples of donors providing funds that helped solve significant environmental problems and had transformative effects from the Environmental Funders Network, Climate Works, and Climate Lead!

The Financial Vehicles of Philanthropic Giving

Whether it's through donations or one-off grantmaking or by establishing a more structured approach like a **Donor Advised Fund (DAF)** or even a **charitable trust** or **foundation**, philanthropy gives us the flexibility to support areas where a financial return isn't the primary goal, but where the potential for positive impact is immense. It's about recognising that some of the most important work in creating a better future needs this kind of dedicated, impact-first approach.

Often, the financial vehicles in philanthropy focus on tax efficiency for high-net-worth individuals, but increasingly, more services and opportunities are available to those of some-net-worth by thinking more strategically about your giving and better understanding the terminology.

Donations

The simplest form of giving vehicle is the **donation**. Broadly defined as voluntary gifts to charitable organisations for public benefit and without the expectation of personal gains, they can take the form of money, goods, services, time, or assets (such as land or shares), and are generally given with few or no conditions on how the gift is used.

There are many ways in which donations are collected. Whether through direct appeals from the charity or through intermediaries that provide a platform for fundraisers, donations can be any amount, in any currency, for any length of time (one-off to ongoing on a monthly or yearly basis). It is up to the donor to decide how much and the frequency of the donations.

Not all charities and not-for-profits are equal in their impact, and not all impactful work needs to be philanthropic. Do consider the impact that occurs across the whole spectrum of capital.

Grants

Whilst the two terms *grant* and *donation* are sometimes used interchangeably, grants tend to be specific amounts of money given to a charity for pre-determined purposes, with expectations outlined in the grant agreement, which specifies budgets, timelines, and expected outcomes. Generally speaking, grants have a formal application and approval process, and certain parameters must be met when using the grant. For this reason, grants are typically administered through established entities such as foundations or other charitable organisations. Grantmaking can also be undertaken outside of more formal structures, and individuals can provide grants for specific activities, charities, or causes. The latter is increasingly seen in the climate action space, where funders recognise the value of flexible, trust-based support to individual change-makers.

Charitable Trusts/Foundations

The terms 'trust' and 'foundation' are used interchangeably in the UK, but they have very slight legal differences. A charitable trust is a legally binding arrangement where one or more individuals (the trustees) hold assets for exclusively charitable purposes that provide a public benefit. A foundation is a separate legal entity, often incorporated, that owns and manages assets for a specific purpose. No, we aren't entirely sure exactly what these slight differences mean either! A trust/foundation is a way to dedicate assets irrevocably to good causes, separate from personal or business interests. Unlike private trusts, charitable trusts/foundations are regulated by the Charity Commission and must demonstrate that their activity falls within the defined charitable purpose.

Whilst foundations and trusts can be a fantastic way of redistributing wealth in line with the founder's wishes, they can be resource-intensive: they usually require staff, and must adhere to certain charity-related codes of conduct, including annual reporting. There are restrictions in place to ensure they have certain structures to oversee the work that they do, including boards of trustees, and increasingly, advisory panels with lived experience of the issues they address, who can help shape and guide their giving strategies.

Donor Advised Funds (DAF)

DAFs offer many of the benefits of charitable trusts/foundations, without the expense, hassle, and responsibilities that come with them (e.g., administration, reporting, and fiduciary responsibilities). DAFs can be funded with a variety of assets (e.g., shares, cash, non-cash assets), which are then ring-fenced for charitable giving. They are designed for immediate tax efficiency, reducing the administrative management of grantmaking for you as the donor.

The funds are managed by a separate entity, typically an umbrella charitable organisation, and as such, the donor cedes financial control of the assets in the fund but can request that the funds be invested, gifted, or granted at any time, to whatever charity the donor chooses. The money can sit in the account as long as the donor likes, but any withdrawals must be for charitable purposes. Until the money is distributed to a charity, it is invested in wealth management products like ETFs or stocks. Generally, DAFs will have a minimum opening balance or require additional contributions on an annual basis. For example, the Charity Aid Foundation (CAF) offers DAFs for donors giving £25,000 or more per year.[13] There is more information on DAFs on the Philanthropy Impact website, together with a list of DAF providers in the UK.

Collective Giving (Pooled Funds)

This is a growing area of philanthropic giving that differs from DAFs in that grantmaking is made in a collective manner. Providing an effective and flexible way of enabling donors to create targeted and strategic grants, pooled funds can give large sums to causes by bringing individual donations together under one grant. The funds can either be fully independent or fiscally hosted by a larger organisation. There has been a trend towards the development of 'pooled funds' (otherwise known as funder collaboratives or intermediaries) such as Farming the Future, where donors (foundations and individuals) pledge money into one fund focused on a specific theme or community.

Whilst collective giving fosters an environment of shared learning, and generally, experts are on hand to help choose the projects that receive support, they can have their limitations, including inadequate resourcing for setup and maintenance, conflict between different funders with regards to the focus of the fund, and a reluctance amongst funders to cede control.

---

[13] Charities Aid Foundation DAF for 2025 - noncash assets. Personal Giving. Retrieved from https://www.cafonline.org/personal-giving/

EXPLORE MORE

Philanthropy Advisers

To find philanthropy advisers in your area, you can search the STEP database. Choose 'philanthropy' for the 'practice area.'

Visit: www.step.org

Employer Giving Schemes

Give As You Earn or Payroll Giving allows you to donate to charities directly from your payroll. Donations are deducted from your pay cheque directly from your employer, which makes the donation tax-efficient for you because it reduces your tax liability. The funds are placed in a separate account available to you to distribute when you want to allocate a donation.

This vehicle is only available through your employer, and the employer is responsible for setting up and administering the programme. Specialist payroll giving agencies assist companies with this service. Employers sometimes treat this vehicle as an added benefit for their employees' well-being, helping charitable causes that their employees support. It can be coupled with other support, such as match-giving or volunteer days.

Think Like An Investor!

Use the same disciplines that you do for selecting other investments (e.g., a trustworthy organisation and team). Even a comparatively small amount of funding can have a tangible impact, particularly when it can be used to leverage much larger amounts from other sources.

Bridging Loans and Concessional Finance

Like many businesses, non-profit organisations can experience challenges with cash flow when facing unforeseen financing gaps – for example, when contract payments are delayed. This can be addressed through the provision of short-term lending or **'bridging' loans,** which can enable the ongoing provision of vital services as and when they are required, rather than waiting for funding to be in place first. This is the approach taken by humanitarian charities such as UNICEF, as well as through initiatives such as the Open Road Alliance, which work to overcome complications of other forms of lending with bridging loans, such as a tendency for lenders to hide and hike lending rates and fees. In the UK, bridging loans have been used very successfully in recent years to help conservation organisations buy land and protect nature.

Concessional loans enable borrowing at below-market interest rates and/or over longer periods of time. For example, women-led agri-businesses and farmers in the Global South can struggle to access affordable finance on account of gender norms, the lender's risk appetite towards agriculture, and other factors. Concessional loans, when provided alongside grants and capacity building support, can therefore help women access the training and equipment they need, as well as develop a track record and credit rating to secure finance in the future. Examples include The Rallying Cry, One Acre Fund, and Root Capital.

DAFs have received criticism for their lack of accountability and transparency, and their misappropriation for tax avoidance. Large sums can be donated to DAFs for immediate tax relief, but there is no regulation regarding when those funds must be spent, meaning they can be 'hoarded' for interminable amounts of time.

It is therefore advisable if you are considering setting up a DAF to secure a value-aligned sponsor, such that any investments made from the DAF align with your aims, ensuring that investments made through the DAF are not undermining the good that is being done through the charitable giving that it enables.

Who's Who in Philanthropy

Different types of organisations of varying sizes and activities form the rich tapestry of the third or voluntary sector. In addition, umbrella or intermediary organisations exist to support and strengthen charities themselves or to support donors, and these are referred to as charity or philanthropy' infrastructure organisations'. When funding environmental causes as an individual, you may come across these different actors who can play various roles in your purposeful journey.

There are four main legal structures of charities in the UK, defined by the Charity Commission (or Scotland's Scottish Charity Regulator): Charitable Incorporated Organisations (CIO); Charitable Company or Community Interest Companies (CIC); Unincorporated Associations; and Trusts.[14] It's helpful to recognise the differences because the different structures can potentially play a role in how you decide to fund. For example, we often look to maximise our donation with an additional 25% boost of Gift Aid. If Gift Aid does not apply, then we can factor that information into our investment.

---

[14] Charity Commission. (n.d.). Charity types: how to choose a structure. GOV.UK. Retrieved from https://www.gov.uk/guidance/charity-types-how-to-choose-a-structure#types-of-charity-structure

EXPLORE MORE

Gift Aid Explained

Gift Aid is a UK government scheme that allows charities to reclaim tax on donations made by UK taxpayers. Essentially, for every £1 donated, the charity can claim back 25p from HM Revenue & Customs (HMRC), effectively increasing the value of the donation by 25% at no extra cost to the donor.

Not only does Gift Aid offer the added benefit to the charity, but higher-rate taxpayers can directly benefit from claiming back tax. If you pay income tax at a rate higher than the basic rate (currently 20%), you can personally claim back the difference between the higher rate you pay and the basic rate on your gross (pre-tax) donation.

For example, if you're a 40% taxpayer and donate £100, the charity claims £25 in Gift Aid, making the gross donation £125. You can then claim back the additional 20% tax (£125 x 20% = £25) through your Self Assessment tax return or by contacting HMRC to adjust your tax code.

Source: https://www.gov.uk/donating-to-charity/gift-aid

Charitable Incorporated Organisations (CIO)

Plain and simple, CIOs are commonly known as charities. These are the organisations that can receive donations and collect Gift Aid. Charities are required to have a governing board of trustees and a constitution. Many are volunteer-led and operated, while larger organisations will employ paid staff. Depending on the size of the organisation, fundraising is often led by the CEO, who will be the first point of contact for donors.

Charitable Companies/Community Interest Companies (CIC)

CICs are limited companies, operating in the same way as any other company, but their primary purpose is to serve their community and have a public benefit rather than private profits. A CIC maintains a separate identity, protecting its directors from liabilities and allowing the company to exist with changes to its board. It also has flexibility in its ability to borrow and generate funds, but cannot qualify for Gift Aid or tax exemptions like its CIO counterparts.

Charitable Trusts and Foundations

Trusts and foundations come in many different forms, with the main difference between the two being that 'trusts' do not have to be officially registered to exist; they are more of an agreement between two parties pertaining to a transfer of assets that are subsequently used for charitable purposes. Meanwhile, foundations own their assets from the outset, and have more flexibility in regards to the activities they undertake. Trusts and foundations tend to adopt a strategic or geographical focus aligned with the founder's or the trustees' areas of interest, for example, supporting communities displaced by climate change, although some support all charitable causes.

Corporate Foundations are generally funded by a specific business and those who work within it, and tend to support local causes in the communities where they work. There are also **family foundations,** which tend to focus on longer-term, intergenerational giving.

As an individual donor, you can find that foundations are helpful partners that provide a broader understanding of what trends and actions are happening in the sector. You can join them to support their work, providing the needed capital to accomplish more progress.

Intermediaries/Philanthropic Advisers

Philanthropic advisers act as non-profit consultants who can support you to make considered, targeted, and impactful decisions with your money. This is a fantastic option for anyone who is daunted by the challenge of approaching environmental philanthropy and the wealth of information that accompanies it.

Specialist philanthropy advisers such as Impatience Earth can help guide your philanthropic journey by facilitating learning journeys with experts on climate and environmental issues that you are interested in, by helping you understand the links between causes you already support and climate change - for example education, gender, and health – and by exploring the various ways in which your philanthropy can be used to drive impact in that space. This can include anything from 'sounding board' style advice to the co-creation of philanthropic strategies, including recommendations with regard to giving mechanisms and potential grantees.

Intermediaries, also referred to as Development Managers, offer a range of philanthropic services, including management of donor advised funds and charitable giving accounts. These services often work closely with employers to run their payroll and match-giving schemes.

EXPLORE MORE

Project Drawdown

Impatience Earth appears alongside other organisations and recommended resources on Project Drawdown.

Visit: projectdrawdown.org

Strategies for Giving

Unlike other forms of investing, philanthropy does not generate returns on investment for the giver, but it does provide a much more valuable social return. It can act as much-needed 'catalytic capital' or 'risk capital' that enables projects and initiatives that benefit society to get off the ground, and to secure additional investment from elsewhere. This approach has been especially important in supporting early-stage **climate adaptation** projects, including those that are trialling new approaches towards addressing the impacts of climate change, such as extreme heat and drought.

Choosing the right charity and mechanism for giving can seem difficult, especially when you are short on time and can't do a deep dive into every cause you care about. Giving often becomes 'ad hoc' and separated from an investment strategy. However, there are a few strategies we use to integrate giving into our overall spectrum of capital strategy.

- **Basic due diligence:** this need not be onerous - you can look up the charity free of charge on the Charity Commission website, or on Giving is Great, you can look for the charity's own annual report to understand its recent activities and impact, and you can look for a Theory of Change or programme evaluation reports.
- **Look for opportunities to give more:** This can either be through employer matching schemes or matched-funding campaigns, like the Big Give's Raise: Earth Fund.
- **Join others**: Whether it's adding your donation to a larger fund or participating as a member of a funding community, you can stretch your impact further with confidence that others are supporting the same issues.

- **Consider the Core**: It's important to know that charities do operate like businesses in that they have the same operating expenses and require revenue to cover those expenses in order to deliver their impact. Charities can really benefit from funding they can use as they see fit, rather than money with lots of strings attached. This is often referred to as **unrestricted or core funding**.
- **Make long-term commitments**: similar to our relationship with our financial advisers, we value getting to know an organisation, which takes time and effort from both parties. When we, as donors, commit to 3 or 5 years of funding, it demonstrates our interest in their work. If we liken grants to community shares, where we don't expect to see a return for 5-7 years, then we can help the charity think more strategically about its future as well.

DID YOU KNOW?

UK's Charity Sector by Numbers

The UK had 170,171 registered charities in June 2024. At least another 20,000 not-for-profit organisations have charitable status but don't feature on the register.

The voluntary sector contributed approximately £18bn to the UK's economy in 2020/21, or 0.8% of GDP.

Micro charities and small charities (defined by an income of less than £10,000 and £10,000 to £100,000 respectively) make up over 80% of the sector*

Currently, just 2% of global philanthropic giving goes towards 'climate mitigation' (reducing and removing the greenhouse gas emissions), which is eight times the funding that climate 'adaptation' receives (responding and adapting to the impacts of climate change).

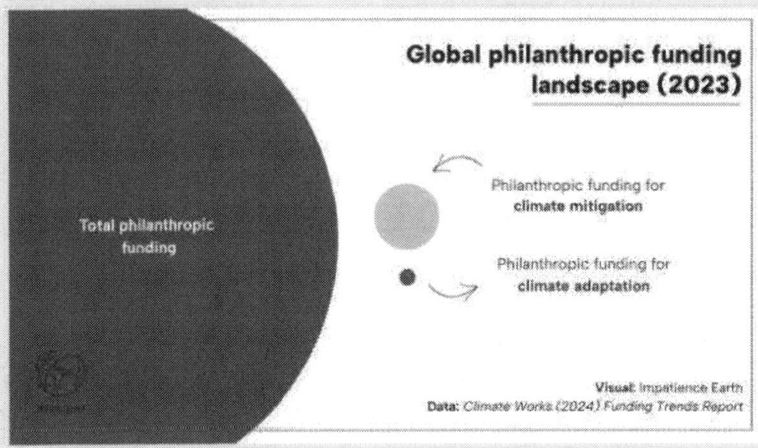

*source: http://policybee.co.uk/blog/uk-charity-statistics

- **Think impact first, taxes second**: So much of our philanthropic planning is geared toward our taxes (or perhaps, avoiding them). When you're able, ask what interests you about supporting the charity, then look at ways that tax efficiencies can enable that outcome.
- **Act fast**: You have the power to be nimble and quick that funding institutions do not. They are burdened with regulatory requirements or internal decision-making processes. Take advantage of your flexibility and go for it!
- ***Where*** **and** ***how*** **matters too**: There is a growing trend toward supporting initiatives and organisations that help shift decision-making power and trust towards the frontline communities who are facing the worst impacts of the climate crisis, and who are therefore best-placed to address them.

We participate in Impact London Collective, knowing that their rigorous due diligence has vetted the organisations for grants, and we are members of the UK's environmental funding community, the Environmental Funders Network.

Media Mania vs Good News

There is no question that charities are held to a higher standard of conduct. But oftentimes, stories of misconduct are misconstrued or inflamed by disinformation in today's online media that outweighs the actual good work from the sector. Yes, scandals do happen (as they do in every sector), but don't be cynical - apply your good analytical skills to read beyond the headlines and understand the issues.

EXPLORE MORE

Trends in Global Climate Giving

Globally, philanthropic giving is on the rise, with an estimated US$885 billion being given to all causes by individuals and foundations worldwide in 2023 - a 10% increase on 2022. For the first time since 2020, Climate Works Foundation identified a growth in climate-related giving, which outpaced overall growth in philanthropic funding in 2023 with a 20% increase from the previous year. A similar trend was identified in the giving of UK-based foundations, with giving towards environmental causes almost trebling between 2021 and 2022. Emerging stories of action collated by the Environmental Funders Network demonstrate that all philanthropic donations - no matter how big or small - have the potential to make a substantial difference.

As well as an increase in the volume of philanthropic giving towards environmental causes*, there has also been a transformation in recent years in regards to the way that we give, in part driven by the rise in the global youth movement which has placed scrutiny over where philanthropic funds are coming from, as well as how they are being redistributed, and to whom.

As such, philanthropists (both at an individual and foundation level) are being called on to take a justice-centered approach towards their giving, addressing historic power imbalances between funders and grantees, and supporting initiatives and organisations that help shift decision-making power and trust towards the frontline communities who are facing the worst impacts of the climate crisis, and who are therefore best-placed to address them. This includes a trend towards the provision of 'unrestricted funding' (which enables the grantee to determine how funds are spent), 'core funding' (which supports operations, including staff salaries), and longer-term, multi-year grants, in recognition of how long it takes to deliver sustained and sustainable change.

*For the first time since 2020, Climate Works Foundation identified a growth in climate-related giving, which outpaced overall growth in philanthropic funding in 2023 with a 20% increase on the previous year. A similar trend was identified in the giving of UK-based Foundations, with giving towards environmental causes almost trebling between 2021 and 2022.

‘Start where you are. Use what you have. Do what you can.’

Arthur Ashe

Questions to Ask

Our 'Wealth with a Why' journey started by being overly curious about what we have and what we want for our future. We've gathered questions and considerations for each of the three areas on the spectrum that worked for us. Find questions that work for you to inform and prepare yourself, or plan your actions.

And, we are not alone on this journey. Use these questions as conversation starters with your advisers, businesses, entrepreneurs, charities, and friends to help you along your purposeful journey.

'My Why' Questions

- **What are my core values when it comes to social and environmental issues?** Get really clear on what matters most to you – is it tackling climate change, promoting social justice, supporting ethical businesses, or something else entirely? This will be your compass.
- **What does 'purposeful' truly mean to *me* in the context of my wealth?** This is a personal question, but reflecting on your values will guide all your decisions.

- **Beyond financial returns, what kind of impact do I want my money to have in the world?** Do you want to avoid supporting harmful industries? Actively invest in solutions? Or perhaps a bit of both?
- **Am I comfortable with the potential trade-offs between financial return and social/environmental impact?** While many believe you don't always have to sacrifice returns, it's good to be clear on your priorities and understand the spectrum of capital.
- **What does 'purposeful giving' mean to me?** Reflect on your personal values and how you want **your generosity** to manifest in the world. What do I have to give of my 5Ts?

Traditional Wealth Management Questions

ASK YOURSELF:

- **How comfortable am I with potentially different levels of financial return if it means achieving greater positive impact?** This is a crucial consideration. Impact investments can have a broad range of financial and impact goals.
- **Across all my financial holdings (bank accounts, pensions, ISAs, investments), where is my money currently held, and what could it be funding?** It's good to get a baseline understanding of your current financial footprint.
- **How important is it for me to know that my investments are creating a tangible, positive difference (additionality)?** This will help determine if you want to explore impact investing more deeply.
- **Am I willing to actively engage with my wealth manager and financial institutions to push for more sustainable options?** Your voice as a client can be powerful.
- **What level of complexity and research am I comfortable with when it comes to understanding the ethical and**

sustainable credentials of my investments? This will influence the types of investment vehicles you might consider.

ASK YOUR WEALTH MANAGER OR YOUR FINANCIAL ADVISER:

Setting and sharing an agenda in advance of meetings will ensure the matters that are important to you and which you wish to discuss are not rushed, and attention inevitably starts to fade. It will also give your adviser time to research or prepare if necessary, making it more likely that you can have an informed discussion. You may be asking questions or making suggestions that your adviser has never encountered before, and they will appreciate not being "put on the spot."

Questions for Your Wealth Manager

- **Do you offer investment strategies that explicitly consider ethical, social, and environmental (ESG) factors?** Don't just accept a 'yes' – dig deeper.
- **How do you define 'sustainable'?** Understand their criteria and if they go beyond basic ESG integration.
- **Can you explain your firm's approach to sustainable and responsible investing?** Understand their philosophy and how it translates into investment choices.

- **What options do you have for screening out harmful investments based on my values (e.g., fossil fuels, tobacco, arms)?** Ask about their exclusion policies and revenue thresholds.
- **Do you integrate ESG analysis into your standard investment selection process, or is it only for clients who specifically ask for it?** This shows how central sustainability is to their approach.
- **Can you give me examples of when ESG considerations have influenced your investment decisions (e.g., not buying a certain stock or selling due to ESG concerns)?** This helps gauge the practical application of their ESG approach.
- **Do you offer 'sustainable' or 'best-in-class' investments that intentionally seek out companies with strong sustainability characteristics?** Try to be as clear as possible with what you would consider 'best'.
- **Are you familiar with thematic investing focused on long-term environmental and social trends (e.g., clean energy, sustainable agriculture)?** This can be a way to actively invest in solutions.
- **Do you offer any impact investment options that aim to create measurable positive social and environmental impact alongside financial returns? If so, can you explain how 'additionality' is created and measured?** Be wary of greenwashing and push for concrete examples.

- **Are you a signatory to the UN Principles for Responsible Investment (PRI) or other relevant sustainability initiatives?** This can indicate a commitment to responsible investment practices.
- **What is your approach to stewardship? Do you actively engage with the companies or fund managers you invest in to encourage sustainability improvements? Do you have a stewardship policy and escalation strategy?** Active ownership is important for driving change.
- **Can you provide sustainability reporting on my portfolio, such as carbon footprint, alignment with net-zero goals, or other relevant metrics? How are these figures calculated, and what do they actually mean?** Transparency is key to understanding the impact of your investments.
- **What are the fees associated with your sustainable and impact-focused investment options compared to your traditional offerings?** Understand the cost implications.
- **Do you have in-house sustainability specialists or rely on external partners for ESG expertise?** This can indicate the depth of their knowledge.
- **Have you received any independent evaluations or accreditations for your sustainability capabilities?** Third-party validation can be helpful.

As part of the typical investing process, an adviser will often expect you to answer around 20 questions about how you would react to the value of your investments going up and down. It is not unreasonable for you to ask them how they will approach the risks that personally concern you.

Questions for Your Financial Adviser

There are three options that you may encounter when working with a financial adviser:

1. *They offer no ethical, sustainable, or impact investment options.*
2. *They offer the above investment options, which they have created in-house.*
3. *They select options or partner with investment management firms to serve their clients' values-based investment needs.*

If **option 1** *applies and you wish to invest in line with your values, then you either need to change your adviser or make your adviser change! With* **option 2**, *the questions for wealth managers work well. For* **option 3**, *where an adviser offers investment funds, portfolios, and products managed by other firms, the following questions are useful:*

- **How many options do you have in your core investment proposition for clients who want to invest in line with their values or have a positive impact?**

- **How and why have you selected the investment providers that you work with?**
- **Do you facilitate bespoke options for clients with more specific ethical investment preferences or who wish to have an impact in a focused area?**
- **How do you determine which options are suitable for which clients?**
- **What are the key differences between the sustainable portfolios you offer: from a cost, risk, performance basis, or positive impact/avoidance of harm basis?**
- **How often do you review the products available to you, and how have your sustainable and impact investment options evolved?**
- **Typically, what percentage of your clients invest in ESG, sustainable, or impact solutions? How do you see this changing in the future?**
- **How much information can you give me about my fund or portfolio? Will I receive any data about alignment with environmental and social outcomes?**
- **Are you able to find out about all the underlying companies held in the funds or portfolios?**
- **How do you assess whether or not investment providers are guilty of greenwashing?**

- **Which of the investment solutions you use has one of the sustainability fund labels, and what is the reason for those that don't have labels?**
- **Can you help me with philanthropic or charitable giving?**
- **Has the firm ensured that its advisers are knowledgeable about sustainability issues and sustainable, ESG, and impact options? When did you last undergo training in this area?**
- **What is your firm's view on climate and nature risks, and how do these affect future investment returns? How do you seek to mitigate this?**
- **What steps have you taken as a firm to have a positive environmental or social impact in your profession or amongst your local community?**
- **How do you think the finance profession can do better to deliver positive social and economic outcomes?**

By asking these kinds of questions, you can start a meaningful dialogue with your wealth manager or financial adviser and ensure that your financial strategy aligns with your desire for a more purposeful and sustainable future. Don't be afraid to challenge jargon and demand clear, understandable answers. Remember, it's your money, and you have the right to understand how it's being used and the impact it's having.

Impact Investment Questions

ASK YOURSELF:

- **Beyond just avoiding harm, what kind of positive impact am I actively seeking to create?** Do you want to directly fund projects with clear additionality? Support enterprises with a strong enterprise impact? Or contribute to broader systemic change?
- **How important is it for me to see clear and measurable outcomes from my impact investments (impact reporting)?** What kind of metrics would give me confidence that my money is making a real difference?
- **How much of my overall portfolio am I prepared to allocate to impact investments?** Think about the scale of change you want to contribute to and how this fits with your broader financial goals.
- How much time and effort am I willing to put into researching and understanding the impact credentials of potential investments? Being an informed investor helps to avoid greenwashing.

ASK THE ORGANISATIONS YOU INVEST IN:

Direct investments will provide you with publicly available information, but you can use these questions to query further when speaking directly to the entrepreneur or platform:

- **What is your organisation's core mission, and how does it directly address the social or environmental issue(s) I care about?** Ask for specifics and avoid vague statements.
- **What are your intended social and/or environmental outcomes?** What are your key performance indicators (KPIs) for impact?
- **How do you measure and report on your social and environmental impact (impact reporting)?** Ask for examples of past reports and how they demonstrate tangible results. What methodologies do you use? Are these reports independently verified?
- **What is your approach to ensuring additionality?** How does my investment contribute to an impact that wouldn't have happened otherwise?
- **What is your organisation's governance structure, and how are ethical considerations embedded in your decision-making processes?**

- **Can you explain your business model and how it aligns with your impact goals?** Is the pursuit of profit intrinsically linked to positive impact (enterprise impact)?
- **What are the potential risks, both financial and impact-related, associated with my investment?** Understand the full picture.
- **How do you ensure transparency and accountability in your operations and impact measurement?**
- **What kind of investor engagement do you encourage?** Will I receive regular updates on your progress and impact?
- **If you are claiming to align with certain sustainability frameworks (e.g., UN Sustainable Development Goals), can you demonstrate how your work contributes to these?**

ASK YOUR WEALTH MANAGER/FINANCIAL ADVISER:

- **What is your experience and expertise in impact investing?** Do you have specific training or qualifications in this area?
- **Please explain the difference between impact investing and other forms of responsible investing, like ESG integration or sustainable investing.**
- **What specific impact investment opportunities do you offer that align with my values and impact goals?** Don't just accept generic 'green' or 'social' funds.

- **How do you assess the social and environmental impact of the impact investments you recommend?** Do you rely on your own analysis or third-party research? How do you avoid greenwashing?
- **Can you explain how additionality is considered when selecting impact investments?**
- **What impact reporting will I receive on my impact investments?** How frequently and in what format? Can you help me understand the data?
- **What due diligence do you perform on the impact credentials of the organisations or funds you recommend?**
- **What is your understanding of intentionality in impact investing, and how do you ensure the investments you recommend are genuinely aiming for specific positive outcomes?**
- **Are you familiar with different impact measurement frameworks and standards?**
- **What are the fees associated with your impact investment offerings compared to traditional investments?** Are they transparent and justifiable?
- **Can you provide examples of successful impact investments you have recommended to other clients and the impact they have achieved?**

- **What is your firm's overall commitment to sustainable and impact investing?**
- **Are you a signatory to any relevant initiatives like the UN PRI?**

By asking these questions across the board, you'll be well-equipped to make truly purposeful impact investments that align with your values and contribute to a more sustainable and thriving future. Don't hesitate to push for clear answers and evidence – your money has the power to make a real difference!

Don't go it alone!

Use investor clubs, with members' shared experience and expertise, to help navigate due diligence. They are also potentially more efficient use of time, beneficial for entrepreneurs, who don't have to face individual questioning from many different interested potential investors.

Philanthropic Giving Questions

ASK YOURSELF:

- **What kind of change am I hoping to see as a result of my philanthropic contributions?** Am I looking for immediate relief, long-term systemic change, or something in between? Think about the impact you want to have.
- **How important is it for me to understand the effectiveness of the organisations I support and the impact they are having?** Do I want to see reports and evidence of the difference my money is making, or am I willing to trust the organisation will achieve its aims without the need for direct reporting?
- **Am I interested in simply making donations, or am I open to more strategic forms of giving, like venture philanthropy or setting up a donor-advised fund?**
- **How much of my capital (my 5Ts) am I prepared to dedicate to philanthropic activities?** Consider not just the amount of money, but also the time and effort you might want to contribute.

ASK THE ORGANISATIONS YOU SUPPORT:

Due diligence can begin with publicly available information from websites or their publications. The Charities Commission hosts a searchable register of all registered charities that provides basic information, which you can then delve deeper into conversation with the charity to learn more.

- **What is your organisation's mission and why?** What problems are they addressing? Ask for a clear and concise explanation of their core purpose.
- **Can you articulate your specific goals and how you measure your success in achieving them?** What are your key performance indicators (KPIs) for social or environmental impact? What else is important to you in terms of measuring and understanding the impact of the work you do?
- **How does my donation contribute to outcomes that wouldn't happen otherwise?**
- **Who is on your senior leadership team?** Learning more about the staff or trustees gives insight into how the organisation is run.
- **Can you provide examples of the impact you have achieved with previous funding?** Ask for data, stories, or reports that demonstrate their effectiveness.

If due diligence and research aren't your strengths, find others who do enjoy the process. Join others with your giving. This is where collective philanthropy is at its best! It's a community, learning, and fun all rolled into one.

- **What is your organisation's governance structure? How are decisions made about the use of philanthropic funds in line with the structure?** Organisations may have explored different business models to best fit their mission.
- **How do you ensure transparency in your operations and the use of donations?** Are your financial reports readily available?
- **What kind of relationship do you have with your donors? Do you foster relationships among donors?** Will I receive updates on your work and the impact of my contribution?
- **If you collaborate with other organisations, how do you ensure alignment and effective use of resources?**
- **What are your biggest challenges, and how can my support best help you overcome them?** Understanding their needs can help you give more effectively.
- **Are you exploring or using innovative financing approaches like blended finance that might leverage philanthropic capital?**

There can be an unspoken power balance with funders, where charities tend to cater to the wishes of the funder rather than the people, causes, and communities they are supporting. But most charitable organisations are time and cash-poor, with staff stretched thin at the best of times. You can be interested without being demanding: Be respectful of how much time you're asking of the organisation, in line with the size of your donation.

ASK YOUR PHILANTHROPIC ADVISER/DEVELOPMENT MANAGER:

- **What is your experience and expertise in advising on philanthropy, particularly in the areas I am interested in?**
- **Can you help me clarify my philanthropic goals and develop a giving strategy that aligns with my values?**
- **What are the pros and cons of Donor Advised Funds (DAFs) or Charitable Trusts?** Would these vehicles make a good fit for my goals?
- **How do you research and vet potential charitable organisations to ensure their effectiveness and alignment with my goals?** What due diligence processes do you have in place?
- **Can you help me understand how my philanthropic giving can complement my impact investing strategy within the spectrum of capital?**

- **How do you track and evaluate the impact of the philanthropic contributions you advise on?** Can you help me understand the impact of reporting from the organisations I support?
- **Are you aware of opportunities for collective giving or collaborative philanthropic efforts in areas I'm interested in?**
- **Can you advise me on the tax implications and administrative aspects of different philanthropic giving methods?**
- **What are your fees, and how are they structured?** Ensure transparency in costs.
- **Can you provide case studies or examples of successful philanthropic strategies you have helped clients implement?**
- **How do you stay up-to-date on the latest trends and best practices in effective philanthropy?**

By asking these questions, you can approach philanthropy with the same intentionality and focus on purpose that you bring to your investments, ensuring that your giving truly contributes to the positive change you wish to see in the world. Remember, generosity, when guided by purpose, can be a powerful force!

Take your time.

Respect time.

Things take time.

Change takes time.

But change will come.

– Xiye Bastida, from her poem

Think of Yourself as a Tree

PART 3

CAPITAL IN ACTION

Capital in Action

As an engaged and conscious investor, you may be able to spot when different financing is at play and target actions according to which type of capital you're able to deploy. That's when we started having some fun along the spectrum. By seeing what impact our actions have, we can use vehicles that work well for the desired outcome. Here are a few ways we matched impact to a financial tool, but note that the vehicles will potentially have multiple impacts:

Impact	Vehicle
Quick Action Needed:	Bridging Loan
Stability Over Longer Terms:	Government Bond
Recognise Company's Commitment:	Stocks, Shares
Back Innovative and Novel Solutions:	Angel/Venture Capital
Community Ownership:	Community Shares/Bonds
Kickstart Change:	Grantmaking
Participate with Others:	Collective Giving
Envision a Thriving Future for All:	Ethical ISA or Pension
Strengthen Voices of Others:	Legislative Support
Connect to People Around the World:	Micro loans with peer-to-peer lending

Taking this knowledge one step further, we applied the 5Ts (treasure, time, talent, ties, and testimony) across the spectrum. Yes, we make financial capital allocations, and we make human capital allocations. Combined, our allocation of all resources is far more meaningful for us as well as the organisations that hold or receive our money. We now see things differently, where others might miss the connection because we are working across the spectrum. Likewise, we strengthened our relationships with our employers, wealth advisers, grantees, investments, friends, and neighbours simply by being more aware of the impact of all our actions.

Whilst we focus broadly on climate and nature, the same decision-making applies to any cause. Put your unique filters on opportunities that feel right for you.

Our Human Capital in Action

We're continually learning with others to enhance our skills. We've participated in learning communities - such as the Conduit, Acumen Next, and Environmental Funders Network - to learn from global social change leaders; explore innovative approaches to impact investing; and collaborate with funders dedicated to tackling poverty, climate resilience, and nature recovery.

Embracing the 5Ts approach, we've volunteered, joined groups, attended conferences, provided our skills, and shared our stories. Here are a few of our human capital examples:

Time:

- Stephanie volunteers for GoodGym, an organisation that provides help with all kinds of community projects. She packed goodie bags for special events. She even counted bats one night along the River Thames. Her time with GoodGym has helped her connect with more projects and people in her local community.

Talent:

- Stephanie used her education and experience in nonprofit management to write a leadership handbook for Impact Collective London.

Testimony:

- Stuart is an active LinkedIn poster, sharing his stories weekly. He often distills his lessons learned and shares his experiences. He also re-shares posts from our investments' projects and announcements.

Ties:

- Stuart joined Green Angel Ventures to learn more about investment opportunities and found former colleagues who were members as well. His connections have led to fruitful introductions to new investment opportunities for Stuart and his colleagues.

Is there a 6th T for you? <u>Trust</u>. This might be reviewing your sources of information, evaluating your relationships, or trusting in yourself to make change happen.

Our Financial Vehicles in Action

We learned a lot about multiplying the impact of our money—unlocking extra funding, inspiring larger contributions, and maximising support for causes we care about without losing sight of returns. Our choices below are not offered as recommendations, but we hope they inspire you to research what might work for you.

TRADITIONAL WEALTH MANAGEMENT ACTIONS

Changing Bank Accounts:

We opened a new bank account at Triodos Bank because it is a B-Corp that aims to change the financial industry by committing to ethical financing. Their tagline, "our banking and financial services are for individuals who want to change the world," resonated with us and our desire to align our finances with our values.

- We opened the account with £20,000 with a focus on using these funds towards our yearly actionable impact. Even if we did nothing else with that £20,000 other than place it in a savings account at this eco-friendly, community-oriented bank, we felt reassured that our money would be 'doing good.'

- Because our mortgage is tied up in our main bank, we've not yet been able to move all our money to a bank fully aligned with our why. So we've added a bit of time focused on advocating for our existing bank to change its practices and move away from industries we don't support.

<u>Moving Pensions:</u>

Inspired by the Make My Money Matter[15] campaign, we've reviewed, reshaped, and moved our investments and pensions towards more ethical and sustainable funds that align with our values and commitment to positive impact.

- Over his career, Stuart built up a mix of company pensions and ISAs. He consolidated and picked investments that met our long-term plans, such as retirement and family milestones, as well as matched our purposeful investing goals. Just like with any investment, the returns have gone up and down, but we're able to apply patience with a long-term outlook to our trading. We've made some changes too, like moving to a more sustainable fund with Scottish Widows and the Accenture Pension, and selling off some stocks and funds from the SIPP, ISA, and regular investment accounts.

[15] Make My Money Matter campaign closed in 2025. Campaign assets are available to download. Retrieved from https://makemymoneymatter.co.uk/

- Stephanie made the decision to move her pension to a new provider, Pension Bee, because they offered fund choices that were both simpler and clearly identified as socially responsible. This move allowed her to align her pension investments with her values.

  - https://makemymoneymatter.co.uk/[23]
  - https://www.scottishwidows.co.uk/about-us/responsibleinvestment.html
  - https://www.pensionbee.com/uk/climate-plan

<u>Working with Financial Advisers</u>:

Partnering with our financial advisers, we continuously refine our investments through an ESG-inspired traffic light system that we designed, incrementally enhancing our portfolio by adding high-impact stocks and phasing out those with negative effects, driving progress through constant learning and improvement.

- We had moved to Charles Stanley because their model allows for pension and investment accounts to contain individual stocks and funds. Although our assets are publicly traded, it's difficult to know exactly what's in the funds. We found that holding specific stocks allows us to have clearer conversations with our advisers about the whole portfolio. Taking this foundation and adding a traffic light system (green for fully aligned with our why and values; red for assets not aligned and not changing; yellow for in between) was a powerful driver of conversations and asset review to provide the insight necessary to move assets and funds to more green lights over the 5 years we've been doing this.

- https://www.charles-stanley.co.uk/about-us/important-information/our-approach-to-responsible-investing

Working with our Employer:

As we have travelled on this journey, we have thought about all our assets, liabilities, costs, and income. We'd traditionally seen income as a single thing, but we discovered that there are various assets in income to consider in more detail. Most employers think of your pay as remuneration for a job well done, but that doesn't mean we should stop there in terms of what we negotiate and what we do with that remuneration.

- Stuart mainly worked in jobs with a steady monthly salary. We look at this salary in terms of covering our monthly costs and also enabling us to save. Our lens as conscious consumers has informed our spending decisions. In the same way, aligning our savings with our values has helped us be more disciplined with our money and focus on investing it wisely.
- Some years there has been a bonus too, which we look at to spend on a treat, a project, or to invest. Adding our why to conversations and decisions means we have fun and feel good about having some money to use.

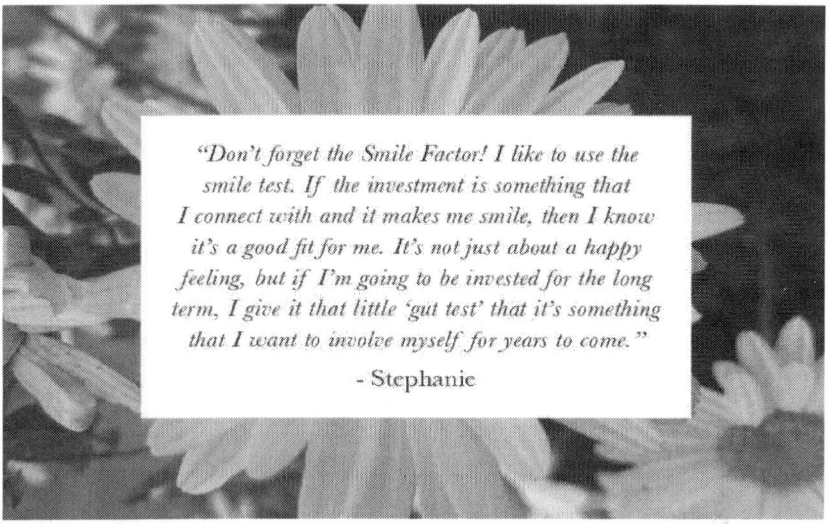

- o In his previous two roles, Stuart received share options. Additionally, we have participated in employee stock purchase programs at prior companies. There are tax benefits and a bunch of details to watch out for in these plans, but overall, we've found them beneficial and an extra incentive to stay with the company. Over the years, we have often let these shares sit, perhaps out of old loyalty, but since rethinking our investments, we've sold shares no longer consistent with our values, to pay for family expenses, and to invest in impact investments. We also moved shares from their workplace programs into our portfolio, so we include their value, risk, and focus in our decision-making.
- ▪ https://us.etrade.com/stock-plans
- ▪ https://www.investopedia.com/terms/e/espp.asp

IMPACT INVESTMENT ACTIONS

***Community Investment*:**

Finding and understanding companies like Energy Garden was no easy feat for us. Luckily, there are platforms that provide rigorous due diligence processes in order to help investors and entrepreneurs create good investment opportunities. We found Ethex not only provided support for our investment purchases but also encouraged us to learn about the 'whys' behind the investments and get to know other investors as well.

- Our investment in Energy Garden is £5,000, and we are projecting a 4-6% per annum return. Investments in Energy Garden start at £50.

- https://www.energygarden.org.uk/community-energy
- https://www.ethex.org.uk/

***Investment Club*:**

We joined the membership and made an investment in the Green Angel Ventures Climate EIS Fund, aiming to align our capital with meaningful climate impact while targeting strong financial returns.

- Our investment in the fund is £15,000, which is invested in 10-15 companies from the Green Angel portfolio. EIS (Income Tax and Capital Gains) tax reliefs are available. The Fund aims to target 3x returns over 5-10 years.

- o Stuart is an active member of the syndicate, which provides access to individual deals. We enjoy being involved in assessing and selecting companies to review with over 350 other investors, learning from their knowledge and experience.
    - https://greenangelventures.com
    - https://greenangelventures.com/invest/eis-climate-change-fund/

<u>Impact Bond</u>:

We made an investment in the Triodos Sterling Bond Impact Fund with the aim of supporting positive environmental and social change, using a financial vehicle where growth has been steady, risk is managed, and funds remain accessible, allowing us to stay agile and invest in emerging opportunities as they arise.

- o Our £5,000 investment has a projected return in 5 years of 25% with an expected impact of 431kg lower footprint of $CO2$ (vs. benchmark funds) and 51kg lower footprint of landfill waste.
    - https://www.triodos.co.uk/impact-investments/sterling-bond-impact-fund

***Microloans*:**

We've made loans as little as $25 per loan through Kiva. Our monthly loans and the repayments keep ticking over and slowly have added up to thousands so far. Our microloans supported people all over the world to start businesses, invest in education, expand farms, and create economic opportunities in their communities.

- Over the years, our 89 small loans (starting at $25) have added up, including relending, to over $3,000. We've supported enterprising people from 36 countries around the world to build their real solutions and helped expand financial access to help underserved communities thrive.
- https://www.kiva.org/about/how

***Crowdfunding Investment*:**

We made an investment in Fishtek Marine through **Triodos Crowdfunding** to support the growth of this fascinating business, aiming to develop innovative bycatch reduction technologies, expand global impact, and drive marine conservation through sustainable fishing solutions.

- Our investment in Fishtek is £1,000 and covered by EIS tax benefits. You can make an investment through Triodod Crowdfunding from £50 and take the opportunity to invest in organisations making a positive impact socially, culturally, and environmentally.
- https://www.triodoscrowdfunding.co.uk/investing

PHILANTHROPIC GIVING ACTIONS

Donations with Employer:

We made donations to organisations such as Médecins Sans Frontières (MSF) and Right to Play through Salesforce's employee matching program, doubling the impact of our contributions and extending our reach to support critical global initiatives.

- Our donations ran from £50 to £500. It all added up, and in seven years, we'd donated over £18,000 and had every pound matched, so charities received another £18,000 from Salesforce. Gift Aid added another 25% for the charities from our giving. Multiplying the impact of our money by 2.25 times! And beyond this, Payroll Giving processed tax benefits for us too.
  - https://www.cafonline.org/corporate-giving/effective-ways-to-give/matched-giving
  - https://www.salesforce.com/company/philanthropy/employee-volunteering-giving
  - https://benevity.com/about-us
  - https://www.gov.uk/donating-to-charity
  - https://www.cafonline.org
  - https://www.cafonline.org/personal-giving/effective-ways-to-give/giving-account/how-does-gift-aid-work

"Introducing ourselves as 'philanthropists' didn't feel right, because after all, philanthropists and investors were mega-rich or super famous people? And that wasn't us, right?

Or, maybe we are philanthropists. The root word philanthropy in Greek translates to 'love of humanity', and the word philanthropist refers to a person who "makes an active effort to promote human welfare." This definition gave us something to get our heads around – that philanthropy was an act for everyone.

By identifying with philanthropy, we take back our agency. We feel more in control of decisions as well as more confident to make the donations at an appropriate time and monetary amount that works for both us and the organisation. With this in mind, referring to ourselves as philanthropists both feels right and makes good sense."

- Stuart

Truly a win-win!

If you are a UK earner, you can increase your donations by 25% through Gift-Aid. It's a tremendous boost for the charity and provides tax benefits to the donor.

***Grants to support the Community*:**

We made a multi-year grant to support Groundwork London's Our Space Award, a small-grants programme that helps communities transform underused spaces into thriving green hubs. It's been amazing to be involved in realising the impact communities gain from their efforts to foster biodiversity, build climate resilience, and enhance social connection.

- Groundwork London stood out because they didn't just acknowledge a donation; they actively engaged with us, inviting further involvement. This early connection led us to participate in the grantmaking programme where we committed to a three-year grant of £5,000 per year to support their Our Space Award and participated in the grantee selection process.
- It has been truly inspiring to visit the recipients of the Our Space Awards and witness firsthand the incredible transformations they are achieving. From creating vibrant community gardens in previously derelict spaces to fostering

biodiversity and building stronger community ties, the impact of these small grants is significant. We appreciate how the programme specifically supports local, unincorporated groups, empowering everyday Londoners to make a lasting difference to their local environment.

- Working with the Groundwork London team has been a rewarding experience. We've learned more about the nuances of supporting green initiatives in our city and seen our contribution benefit so many different community groups.
    - https://www.groundwork.org.uk/london/our-space-award/

<u>Grant through a Platform</u>:

We made a grant through Action Funder to a community centre running financial education workshops. In the process, we not only supported a vital community initiative but also gained invaluable insights into the challenges and responsibilities of grantmaking.

- Although Action Funder hadn't worked with individuals before, they agreed to support us in a trial. The platform listed many projects seeking around £500 in funding, an amount we could cover fully. To use the site, we created a profile and an open fund, which Action Funder then notified relevant organisations about. From over 250 potential matches, Stephanie narrowed it down to five, and ultimately, we funded one £2,000 project run by a community centre providing financial education workshops for 60 participants.
    - https://www.actionfunder.org/

***Collective Giving*:**

We joined Impact London Collective (formerly Impact 100 London) and pooled our donations with others to fund transformative, multi-year grants that empower women and girls in London, ensuring our collective giving creates meaningful and lasting change in our community.

- Stephanie found Impact London Collective to be a far more engaging and impactful approach to giving compared to online grantmaking. She valued how her £1000 contribution was combined with those of 99 other members to create a significant £100,000 grant. This collective power allowed them to fund transformative projects for women and girls in London in a way that individual smaller grants might not achieve. Stephanie also deeply appreciated the sense of community among the members, the opportunity to learn about critical issues facing women and girls in London, and the engaging energy of the member events. This model not only amplified the financial impact of her giving but also provided a richer and more connected philanthropic experience.
  - https://www.impactlondoncollective.org/our-mission

Support Legislative Advocacy:

We made a gift to support Peers for Planet's work on accelerating climate action and biodiversity protection through legislative advocacy, cross-sector collaboration, and parliamentary education, in support of the system-wide change we need to see.

- We'd not considered advocacy work within the UK Parliamentary system until we met Peers for Planet through the Environmental Funders Network. It's easy to think that getting involved in the machinery of legislation needs joining a political party or a job in the civil service. Becoming more involved allowed us to connect with this exceptional team. Their quiet dedication supports legislators in driving change and participating effectively in crucial debates.
- https://www.peersfortheplanet.org/

Good with Money is a great resource to learn more about the different options and how your money works for good.
EARTH.ORG is like a newspaper written by the planet. Its two platforms discover and act are invaluable resources for anyone looking to learn more and do more.

Your Capital in Action

Give it a go! Make a plan for your wealth with your why...

1. Take Stock of Your Wealth

- *Your education*
- *Your skills*
- *Your activities*
- *Your interests*
- *Your connections*

Where do they match up with your values? Where do have have human capital to dedicate to 'your why'? Next, using the spectrum of capital, identify what financial vehicles you currently use, then consider:

· *What you'd like to keep*

· *What could you switch or change*

· *What could you exit*

· *What would you like to add*

As with any financial decision, it helps to be organised and plan ahead when possible.

2. Schedule Your Time

- *Consider the time(s) of year when you can dedicate time to investments*
- *Consider lengths of commitments*
- *Plan conferences and meetings that may require travel or days off work*
- *Schedule an annual MOU - Check in on your values. Take stock of your skills and resources, as they will change over time*

3. Consider your budget

- Have an amount and/or percentage in mind to allocate over the year

4. Set commitments

- *To Yourself!*
- *To Others*
- *To the Planet*

We know that anxiety can be paralysing, especially around climate change. The antidote is action. As Dan Harris says, "Action absorbs anxiety." When we shift from worrying to doing, we take back control.[16] We move from feeling helpless to feeling empowered.

- **Focus on what you can control**: instead of getting bogged down by the things you can't change, channel your energy into taking positive action.
- **Start small if you must, but start**: taking even a small step forward can make a big difference in how we feel.

We've personally found that getting involved in projects that align with our values has been a game-changer for our mental well-being. It's given us a sense of purpose and meaning, and it's helped us feel more connected to something larger than ourselves.

We invite you to join us on this journey and find your joy. We look forward to what we all discover together along the way.

[16] Harris, D. (n.d.). *10% Happier*. Retrieved from https://www.danharris.com/

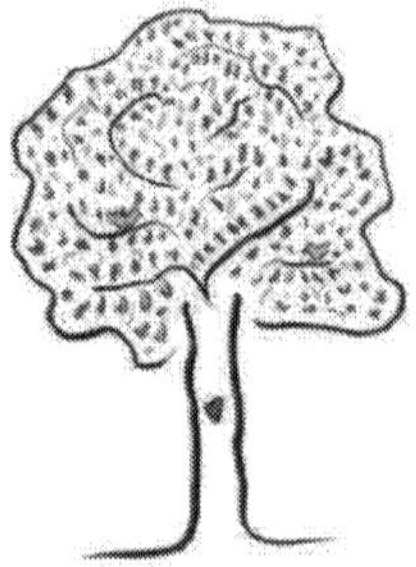

‘The best time to plant a tree was 20 years ago. The second best time to plant a tree is today.’

Chinese Proverb

Appendix

Glossary

Wealth management and philanthropy sectors are jargon-rich. *The words listed below introduce you to many terms you may encounter in your journey. We've added Wealth With a Why references, such as Some Net Worth, 'to Impact Investing Institute's already highly comprehensive list*:

A

- **Additionality**: The positive impact or outcome that would not have occurred without specific investment or intervention.
  - *Example:* A social housing project in Manchester that wouldn't have been built without impact investment funds.
  - *Example:* Financing a new wind farm in Scotland, demonstrating high intensity impact and clear *additionality*
- **Angel Investor**: An individual who invests their own money into startups or small businesses in exchange for equity, typically acquiring a minority stake ranging from 10% to 25%. Angel investors often provide not only financial support but also mentorship and industry expertise, playing a crucial role in the early stages of a business's development.
  - *Example:* A London-based angel investor supporting fintech startups like Monzo in their early stages.

- **Asset Manager**: An investment team or firm tasked with selecting and managing assets in a portfolio or fund on behalf of investors.
  - *Example:* Schroders, a leading UK asset management firm focusing on sustainable investments.

B

- **Blended Finance:** Financing that uses patient risk-tolerant 'catalytic capital', for example from development or philanthropic sources, in order to attract and mobilise additional private capital flows to impact investment opportunities.
  - *Example: Big Society Capital's use of blended finance to support social enterprises across the UK.*
  - *Example: Cazenove Capital's sustainable investment strategies, which may incorporate blended finance approaches to achieve both financial returns and positive impact*
- **B-Corp:** A type of company committed to ethical financing and positive societal impact. B-Corp certification is awarded by B Lab and requires companies to meet high standards of social and environmental performance, accountability, and transparency.
  - *Example:* Triodos Bank, a certified B-Corp operating in the UK.
- **Bridging Loans:** Short-term loans provided to non-profit organisations to address cash flow challenges.
  - *Example:* A charity in Birmingham using a bridging loan to cover expenses while waiting for a large grant payment.

- *Example:* UNICEF and initiatives like Open Road Alliance using bridging loans to manage unforeseen financing gaps

C

- **Capital Markets**: The multi-trillion markets on which companies, governments and other organisations raise large-scale funding by selling financial instruments such as shares and bonds to investors.
  - *Example:* A goal of the Impact Investing Institute is to make capital markets work better for everyone by all capital markets investments being impact-focused.
- **Carbon Neutrality**: Achieving net zero carbon dioxide emissions through a combination of cutting emissions and absorbing or capturing them.
  - *Example:* The UK government's commitment to achieving carbon neutrality by 2050 includes initiatives like planting millions of trees and expanding offshore wind capacity.
- **Catalytic Capital**: Investment capital that accepts higher risk or reduced returns to enable ('catalyse') other third-party investment in a new and unproven opportunity that would otherwise not be possible. Catalytic capital might mitigate risk for other investors by providing a guarantee, taking a higher-risk tranche or a 'first-loss' investment.
  - *Example:* The Esmée Fairbairn Foundation providing catalyst funding for innovative environmental projects in Scotland.
  - *Example:* Gower Street Foundation's funding of Extinction Rebellion.

- **Charitable Trusts / Foundations**: Entities redistributing wealth for charitable purposes, with Trusts being agreements and Foundations owning assets outright.
    - *Example:* The Wellcome Trust, one of the UK's largest charitable foundations supporting medical research.
    - *Example:* The Environmental Funders Network, which supports environmental philanthropy in the UK and Europe
- **Circular Economy:** An economic model aimed at minimizing waste by keeping resources in use for as long as possible through recycling and reusing.
    - *Example:* The Ellen MacArthur Foundation, based in the UK, promoting circular economy initiatives globally.
- **Climate Adaptation**: the ability to adapt to and prepare for the impacts of climate change
    - *Example:* The Thames Barrier in London, designed to protect the city from rising sea levels.
    - *Example:* Retrofitting homes in flood-prone areas of Yorkshire to withstand extreme weather events.
- **Climate Mitigation**: Reducing and removing greenhouse gas emissions.
    - *Example:* The UK's offshore wind farms contributing to the reduction of carbon emissions in the energy sector.
    - *Example:* The UK's Green Homes Grant scheme aimed at improving energy efficiency in residential properties.
- **Collective Giving**: Collaborating with other philanthropists to address issues together, often through pooled funds.
    - *Example:* The London Funders Network coordinating collective giving for COVID-19 response in the capital.

  - *Example:* The Global Methane Hub (GMH), created through a $200 million pledge by philanthropists.
- **Community-based Resilience**: the sustained ability of a community to respond to, withstand, and recover from adverse situations or disruptive challenges, both natural and man-made, sudden or chronic." (The definition was developed by UK-based NGO HOPE not hate.)
- **Community Benefit Society (CBS)**: An organisation operating for the benefit of the community, often using a democratic, one-member-one-vote system.
  - *Example:* Hastings Pier Charity, which raised funds through community shares to restore the local pier.
- **Community Shares**: A method for community organisations to raise finance from individual investors who become voting members.
  - *Example:* The New Leaf Co-op in Edinburgh, which used community shares to establish an ethical grocery store.
  - *Example:* Community renewable energy initiatives listed on Ethex's platform
- **Concessional Loans**: Loans offered at below-market interest rates or over longer periods to support NGOs and their beneficiaries.
  - *Example:* Big Issue Invest providing concessional loans to social enterprises across the UK.
  - *Example:* The Rallying Cry, One Acre Fund, and Root Capital providing concessional loans.
  - *Example:* Social Investment Scotland providing concessional loans to community projects.

- **Co-operative**: A member-owned and democratically controlled organisation formed to meet the common economic, social, and cultural needs of its members. Profits are typically reinvested or distributed among members rather than external shareholders.
    - *Example:* Energy4All is a UK cooperative that enables communities to develop and own renewable energy projects such as wind and solar farms, allowing individuals to invest directly in local clean energy generation.
- **Corporate Social Responsibility (CSR)**: The integration of social and environmental concerns into a company's core business operations.
    - *Example:* Marks & Spencer's Plan A initiative, which aims to make the company the world's most sustainable retailer.
    - *Example:* Cazenove Capital's commitment to responsible investment and sustainable wealth management.
    - *Example:* Unilever UK's commitment to reducing plastic waste through its sustainable packaging initiatives.
- **Co-investment Investing** alongside other investors in a project or fund, often on the same terms.
    - *Example:* A consortium of high-net-worth individuals co-investing in a renewable energy project in Wales.
- **Co-creation Partnership**: An alliance whereby institutional investors and impact investors, including MDBs and DFIs, and others such as foundations, jointly establish an investment vehicle to catalyse capital towards an social or environmental impact objective.
    - *Example:* Better Society Capital and UK foundations collaborated to create the Growth Fund, a co-creation

partnership providing blended finance to social enterprises.

- **Co-management Partnership**: Investment managers with complementary skill sets and expertise, e.g., a mainstream asset manager and an impact manager, cooperate to leverage their respective capabilities to create a combined investment offering that is attractive to institutional investors.
    - *Example:* Schroders and Big Issue Invest partnered to co-manage the Schroders Big Issue Sustainable Fund, combining mainstream asset management with impact expertise.
- **Crowdfunding**: Raising finance by asking a large number of people each for a small amount of money.

D

- **Development Finance Institution (DFI)**: A government-backed institution that invests in private sector projects in low and middle income countries to promote job creation and sustainable economic growth.
    - *Example:* CDC Group, the UK's DFI, invests in African renewable energy projects to promote sustainable economic growth and job creation.
- **Donor Advised Funds (DAFs):** Funds managed by a sponsor for charitable giving, offering benefits similar to Charitable Foundations.
    - *Example: The Charities Aid Foundation (CAF) offering DAFs to UK philanthropists.*

E

- **Emerging Market:** A developing nation that is in the process of becoming an industrialised economy, and can therefore see more rapid rates of economic growth than developed markets.
  - *Example:* UK-based CDC Group investing in African renewable energy projects.
- **Engagement/Shareholder Engagement** Actions taken by shareholders to influence a company's behaviour towards more sustainable practices.
  - *Example:* This might be through voting at companies annual general meeting or by meeting and influencing.
- **Enterprise Impact:** The positive social or environmental effects generated by the products or services provided by a company.
  - *Example:* A social enterprise in London providing job training for disadvantaged youth.
- **Enterprise Investment Scheme (EIS):** A scheme providing tax advantages for some impact investments.
  - *Example:* An investor using EIS to support a renewable energy start-up in Wales.
  - *Example:* Green Angel Ventures using EIS to support early-stage environmental startups.
- **Ethical Bonds:** Funding instruments for organisations committed to positive social or environmental impact, offering interest repayments.
  - *Example:* Retail charity bonds issued by Charities Aid Foundation to support its lending to charities.

- **Environmental, Social, and Governance (ESG):** Factors incorporated into investment decisions to identify risks and opportunities.
    - *Example:* Legal & General Investment Management's Future World funds, which incorporate ESG factors.
    - *Example:* Cazenove Capital's integration of ESG factors into their investment process.
- **Exchange Traded Funds (ETFs):** A form of regulated collective investment fund.
    - *Example: The iShares MSCI UK IMI ESG Leaders UCITS ETF, which tracks UK companies with high ESG ratings.*

F

- **Fiduciary Duty:** The obligation on institutional investors, such as pension fund trustees, to act in the best interest of scheme members. The Impact Investing Institute has worked to show that fiduciary duty and impact investing are compatible.
    - *Example:* The Impact Investing Institute has demonstrated that pension schemes like Nest can align fiduciary duty with impact investing by supporting green infrastructure projects.
- **Financial Conduct Authority (FCA):** The UK regulatory body overseeing financial advice and markets.
    - *Example:* The FCA's introduction of Sustainability Disclosure Requirements for investment funds.
- **Financial Planner:** A professional focusing on establishing financial and life goals with clients.
    - *Example:* A certified financial planner in Leeds helping clients align their investments with their values.

- **Financial Adviser:** A neutral term for firms providing financial advice, emphasising investment management services.
  - *Example:* An independent financial adviser in Glasgow specialising in ethical investment strategies.
- **Fixed Income:** Securities that pay a fixed regular income and return capital to investors at the end of a fixed term. Including government bonds like UK gilts, fixed income plays a key role in funding impact activities.
  - *Example: The Retail Charity Bonds platform offering bonds for charities like Hightown Housing Association.*

G

- **Greenwashing:** The exaggeration of environmental or social impact by companies.
  - *Example:* A UK fast fashion brand claiming sustainability credentials without substantial evidence.
  - *Example:* A UK supermarket chain overstating its use of recyclable packaging without clear evidence.

H

- **High Net Worth (Ultra High Net Worth)**: An individual with more than £1m in highly liquid assets. (ultra high net worth individuals have over £25m)

I

- **Impact-Aligned Collective Investment Funds:** Funds that prioritise impact alongside financial returns.

  - *Example: WHEB Sustainability Fund, focusing on companies solving sustainability challenges.*

- **Impact Investing:** Investments made with the intention to generate positive, measurable social and environmental impact alongside financial returns.
  - *Example:* Big Issue Invest's investment in social enterprises across the UK.
  - *Example:* Impact Shakers' focus on supporting impact-driven startups and entrepreneurs.
- **Impact Reporting:** Evidence of real-world outcomes achieved through impact investments.
  - *Example:* Annual impact reports published by Bridges Fund Management detailing the social and environmental outcomes of their investments.
  - *Example:* Triodos Bank's annual impact report detailing its investments in sustainable agriculture across the UK.
- **Individual Savings Accounts (ISAs):** Tax-advantaged products that can hold various investments.
  - *Example:* A stocks and shares ISA holding ethical funds offered by a UK building society.
- **Innovative Finance ISA (IF ISA):** A tax-free way to invest in alternative finance options like peer-to-peer lending.
  - *Example:* Abundance Investment's IF ISA allowing investments in renewable energy projects.
- **Institutional Investor:** An organisation that invests capital on behalf of its members, policyholders or beneficiaries, with an in-house or third-party asset manager overseeing the day-to-day running of the investment portfolio. Institutional investors include pension funds, insurers, charities and foundations, and

sovereign wealth funds, and comprise the largest investors in the world.

- *Example:* Legal & General Investment Management, a leading UK institutional investor, manages funds incorporating ESG principles to benefit policyholders.

- **Intentionality:** An impact investor's deliberate goal to contribute to specific positive and measurable outcomes.
  - *Example:* A UK pension fund explicitly stating its intention to invest in companies reducing carbon emissions.
- **Investment Bonds:** Tax-advantaged products that can hold pooled funds.
  - *Example:* A bond offered by a UK insurer that invests in a portfolio of ethical and sustainable funds.
- **Investment Trusts:** A form of regulated collective investment fund1.
  - *Example:* The Impax Environmental Markets Trust, investing in companies offering environmental solutions.

J

- **Just Transition:** Moving to a net zero carbon global economy in a way that is fair and inclusive to everyone – at every social level and in every geographic region. A just transition should maximise the opportunities created from moving to more sustainable practices by creating decent work opportunities and leaving no one behind.
  - *Example:* Supporting coal miners in Wales transitioning to renewable energy jobs through targeted investments.
- **Just Transition Financing Vehicles:** Investment funds and other vehicles built expressly to help finance a transition to a

net-zero carbon world that is inclusive and beneficial to society – including by incorporating the Just Transition Elements.

- *Example:* The UK Green Finance Institute launched financing vehicles to support a just transition for communities affected by coal mine closures in Wales.

N

- **Net Zero:** A commitment to balance emissions produced and emissions removed from the atmosphere.
  - *Example:* The UK government's legally binding target to achieve net zero emissions by 2050.

O

- **Open-ended Investment Companies (OEICs):** A form of regulated collective investment fund.
  - *Example:* The Royal London Sustainable Leaders Trust, an OEIC investing in companies with strong ESG credentials.

P

- **Passive Funds:** Funds that mirror or sample the holdings of a market index.
  - *Example:* The HSBC FTSE 100 UCITS ETF, tracking the performance of the UK's largest 100 companies.
- **Patient Capital:** Investment where the investor is willing to commit for the very long term before realising a financial return in order to support early-stage enterprise and innovation or higher-risk investment – typically in order to solve a social or environmental challenge.

    - *Example:* Triodos Bank provides patient capital to early-stage social enterprises in the UK focused on renewable energy and community development.
- **Payroll Giving Scheme:** gives money to charity without paying tax on it, paid through PAYE from someone's wages or pension. The donation must be administered through the employer.
- **Peer-to-peer Lending:** A form of alternative finance that can be invested in through an IF ISA.
    - *Example:* Funding Circle, a UK-based peer-to-peer lending platform for small businesses.
- **Pensions:** Retirement funds that can be invested in various options, including socially responsible choices.
    - *Example:* NEST (National Employment Savings Trust) offering ethical fund options to UK pension savers.
- **Philanthropy:** Using capital to generate positive social and environmental change, often without expecting financial returns.
    - *Example:* The Sainsbury Family Charitable Trusts supporting various causes across the UK.
    - *Example:* The Environmental Funders Network's role in supporting and coordinating environmental philanthropy
- **Place-based Impact Investing (PBII):** The practice of developing real estate assets in specific locations to achieve specific social or environmental objectives, while also targeting a financial return for investors.
    - *Example:* The Bristol City Funds initiative uses PBII to develop affordable housing and community spaces in underserved areas of the city.

- **Pooled Fund:** A professionally managed fund where multiple investors' money is combined.
    - *Example:* The BMO Responsible Global Equity Fund, pooling investments from multiple UK investors.
- **Private Investments:** Asset classes such as private equity, private debt, and infrastructure that aren't traded on public stock markets and can therefore give investors a lot of control to achieve their social and environmental objectives.
    - *Example:* UK-based Bridges Fund Management focuses on private investments in sectors like sustainable infrastructure and healthcare innovation.

R

- **Real Assets:** Refers to investable assets that are tangible – principally property and infrastructure – rather than tradable securities such as equities and bonds.
    - *Example:* The Impax Environmental Markets Trust invests in real assets such as renewable energy infrastructure across the UK.

S

- **Securitisation:** The practice of structuring a financial institution's loan portfolio into securities that can be sold to investors in order to free up capital on the institution's balance sheet for further lending and investment.
    - *Example:* Securitisation is increasingly being used by multilateral development banks and development finance institutions to expand their financing capabilities in the impact investing space.

- **Seed Enterprise Investment Scheme (SEIS):** A scheme providing tax advantages for early-stage impact investments.
  - *Example:* An angel investor using SEIS to support a social tech start-up in Bristol.
- **Social Bonds:** Financial products used by the banking sector to fund impact initiatives.
  - *Example:* Lloyds Bank's £250 million ESG bond to support SMEs in deprived areas of the UK.
- **Social Enterprise:** A social enterprise is a business that prioritises specific public interest objectives over shareholder profits.
- **Some Net Worth**: An individual with significant assets but whose financial decisions are affected by liabilities and variables. Their net worth's stability can be impacted by shifting political and economic changes.
- **Socially Responsible Investment (SRI):** Focusing on systematically screening out harmful products and practices (such as companies involved in tobacco, firearms, or gambling) from an investment portfolio.
  - *Example:* Cazenove Capital screens out tobacco and gambling companies from its SRI portfolios for UK investors seeking ethical options.
- **Spectrum of Capital:** Describes the gradations of financial return vs impact that capital may look to achieve. Ranges from traditional investing, which solely looks to deliver financial return, to impact investing, which looks to achieve both financial return and impact, and, finally, philanthropy, which looks to achieve impact with no expectation of financial return.

   - *Example:* The spectrum used by the UK National Advisory Board on Impact Investing to guide investors.
   - *Example:* Cazenove Capital's range of investment options, from traditional to impact-focused strategies.
- **Stewardship:** Active engagement with invested companies or fund managers to encourage sustainability improvements.
   - *Example:* Legal & General Investment Management's Climate Impact Pledge, engaging with companies on climate change.
- **Sustainability Disclosure Requirements (SDR):** FCA rules for providers of investment funds with environmental and social characteristics.
   - *Example:* A UK asset manager revising its fund documentation to comply with SDR guidelines.
- **Subordinated Capital:** A type of blended capital widely used for impact investment where junior tranches absorb any losses first, so senior tranches are protected from loss - thereby enabling more risk-averse investors to participate.
   - *Example:* Big Society Capital uses subordinated capital to de-risk investments in UK social enterprises, encouraging participation from mainstream investors.
- **Sustainable Investing:** Selecting companies that have the potential to outperform the market because they are managing environmental, social, and governance (ESG) risks and opportunities in a more sustainable way than their peers and are therefore more likely to flourish in a changing landscape.
   - *Example:* Schroders' sustainable multi-asset funds available to UK investors.

  - *Example:* Ethex's platform offering a range of sustainable and ethical investment opportunities.
- **Syndication:** In impact terms, a blended finance transaction where a lead investor such as a multilateral development bank syndicates part of a loan to institutional investors, thereby enabling the latter to participate in development opportunities - for example, in emerging markets.
  - *Example:* The CDC Group syndicated loans with UK institutional investors to fund solar power projects in emerging markets like Kenya.
- **Syndicates (Angel/Investor Clubs)**: a group of individuals or organisations combined to promote a common interest

T

- **Thematic Investing:** Constructing a portfolio based on specific medium to long-term trends.
  - *Example:* The Pictet Clean Energy Fund, focusing on the global transition to renewable energy.
- **Traditional Investing:** The finance-first end of the spectrum of capital, focused on maximising financial returns, without any responsible, sustainable, or impact investing considerations.
  - *Example:* A FTSE 100 tracker fund offered by a major UK bank.

U

- **UN Sustainable Development Goals (SDGs; aka 'The Global Goals'):** A collection of seventeen interlinked objectives adopted by the United Nations designed to serve as a shared blueprint for peace and prosperity for people and the planet.
    - *Example:* Many impact investments will take the SDGs into account in their design.
- **Unrestricted/Core Funding**: Organisations can use funds for operational costs or development as needed without specific expectations or ties to how the money is to be spent.

V

- **Venture Philanthropy:** An approach combining elements of venture capital and philanthropy.
    - *Example:* Impetus-PEF providing financial and non-financial support to charities tackling youth unemployment in the UK.

W

- **Wealth Manager:** A professional managing others' wealth, providing services like investment selection and tax management.
    - *Example:* Wealth managers - such as Cazenove Capital, Rathbone Greenbank, EQ Investors - can have demonstrated commitment to sustainable and impact investing.

Our Partner People

Our talented ties that brought our testimony to life!

Yasmin Ahammad, CEO

Impatience Earth

Yasmin has 15 years experience in international development and social justice, and has been a long-time climate activist. Her work includes supporting indigenous migrants and refugees from Myanmar, as well as grassroots communities on the frontline of climate change across Asia.

- linkedin.com/in/yasmin-ahammad-44023057

Lisa Ashford, CEO and Director

Ethex

With over 20 years of experience in energy and environmental markets, Lisa is a leading voice in the positive investing and social enterprise sectors in the UK. A regular media commentator and writer on her passion for ethical investment, Lisa has led the team at Ethex and our sister platform, Energise Africa to jointly raise over £100 million from investors to support projects that are making a positive difference.

- linkedin.com/in/lisa-ashford-mbe-9491389/

Jane Cabutti, Growing Philanthropy Lead

Environmental Funders Network

She leads the organisation's work to increase philanthropic support for environmental issues. Prior to joining EFN in 2016, she worked for over 20 years in fundraising, for organisations such as Space for Giants, the Earth Trust, NSPCC, Oxfam and a local Wildlife Trust (where she led the early fundraising for the fenland recreation project, the Great Fen).

- linkedin.com/in/jane-cabutti-39160033

Hannah Dillon, Communications Consultant

Impatience Earth

Hannah has experience working in environmental policy, advocacy, and strategic philanthropy. As well as campaigning for the implementation of stronger and more equitable decarbonisation policies in the UK, she has also worked across Indonesia, and is a big advocate for progressive, flexible and community-based philanthropy - with a focus on youth and indigenous people.

- linkedin.com/in/hannah-dillon-369a625b/

Julie Dunn, Marketing Manager and Content Creator

Ethex

Julie has more than 20 years of marketing experience and forms part of the Ethex marketing team responsible for creating compelling content to help more people learn about the fantastic ethical organisations that raise finance through Ethex.

- linkedin.com/in/julie-dunn-5a26855

Sarah Farrell, Director

Impatience Earth

Sarah has worked with both UK and international organisations that deliver social and environmental impact, powered by philanthropy. Prior to Impatience Earth, she worked in climate finance. Her interests include: building community resilience and adaptation and the role of media and communications in climate action.

- linkedin.com/in/sarah-farrell-8aa59376

Melissa Gilmour, Group Head of Marketing

Ethex

A decade of experience in sustainable marketing and communications in the consumer and private investing environment; to support scaling impact investing to reach everyday people and build momentum to make money count for more and do good.

- linkedin.com/in/melissagilmour/

George Harding-Rolls, Public Relations Consultant

Impatience Earth

With years of experience in corporate campaigning and sustainability George has deep experience in creating and supporting campaigns that shift market share away from unsustainable products and companies and towards environmentally and socially beneficial solutions.

- linkedin.com/in/george-harding-rolls/

Sarah Hughes, philanthropy & strategy tech-for-good consultant

Charity 21

Sarah has worked in or adjacent to the social impact sector for three decades in the capacities of founder, consultant, executive leader or mentor. She was previously Executive Director of The Beacon Collaborative working closely with major philanthropists and impact investors. She is a strong advocate of everyday philanthropy and wealth for purpose, and supports the platforms Charizone and Givey as a voluntary advisor. In her spare time she has cofounded a therapeutic music app called Mishi.

- linkedin.com/in/C21sarah/

Alina Klarner, Founding Partner

Impact Shakers

Alina founded Impact Shakers Ventures, a €20mil impact VC fund investing in early-stage impact startups with diverse founding teams in climate tech, inclusion tech, and impact infrastructure across Europe and the UK. She also co-runs the Impact Shakers Microfund, a community-led investment vehicle, is a mentor for various startup programmes, an angel investor in diverse impact founders and leads an Impact Angel Programme for emerging impact investors. Prior to joining Impact Shakers, Alina spent over a decade in Advisory Services and Private Equity.

- linkedin.com/in/alinaklarner/

Rebecca Kowalski, FPFS

Good Stock & **Unburdened Solutions**

Rebecca has been working for financial advice firms in Scotland since the 1990s. She is qualified as a Chartered Financial planner and has specialist knowledge in sustainable investment. Rebecca's interest in sustainable finance stems from her environmentalist daughter's concerns about the climate and nature crises. She believes that the finance profession has the ability and responsibility to add its skills and voices to the call for urgent climate action.

- linkedin.com/in/rebecca-kowalski-overstory

Sophia Omar, Programme Manager

Impact Investing Institute

Sophia leads initiatives to embed environmental and social impact at the core of investment decision-making. She has campaigned to clarify UK pension trustees' fiduciary duty, delivered targeted programming to mobilise private wealth towards impact investment, and led direct advisory work with foundations and family offices managing over £1.8 billion in assets. Her work spans coalition building, policy research, and technical advisory, with a particular focus on climate finance and systemic investment. Sophia holds a BA from King's College London and a Certificate in Impact and Impact Investing from CFA UK. She also serves as a judge for the Africa Impact Investing Awards and sits on the Finance and Investment Committee of the Barnwood Trust.

- linkedin.com/in/sophia-o-24b704124

Emilie Shaw, Sustainable Solution Lead

Cazenove Capital

Emilie's 13 years' experience helping Charities, Universities, Individuals and Family Offices align their investment portfolios with their values and to invest for a better future for people and the planet. Emilie leads the sustainable solutions division, and is a chair on the Sustainable Investment Committee, which oversees c.£5bn of investment on behalf of Cazenove Capitals clients, and is co-manager of the Charity Sustainable Multi-Asset Fund. Emilie holds the CISI Chartered Wealth Manager Qualification, Securities and Derivatives certificate and the Investment Management Certificate (IMC).

- linkedin.com/in/emilie-shaw-mcsi-32714659

Dr Alan Whittle MSc MA FPFS

Unburdened Solutions

A great believer in lifelong learning, Alan is a Chartered Financial Planner and Fellow of the Personal Finance Society who holds an MSc in Financial Planning and Business Management. He also holds specialist qualifications in Impact Investing, Investment Management, Financial Crime, Risk Management, Green Finance and Climate Risk. Alan was awarded a PhD in Financial Planning by Manchester Metropolitan University in February 2025. The subject of his thesis was how reference points, frames and framing impact investment decision-making in advised Impact Investing. His continued research interests are primarily in the fields of social and responsible investing, what motivates people to invest, and applied ethics in a financial services context.

- linkedin.com/in/alan-whittle-phd-msc-fpfs-129aa01b/

Resources

It's a mere drop in the ocean to what is available, but Wealth With A Why contains over a hundred references to outstanding material that informed our thinking. Visit www.wealthwithawhy.co.uk for our full list of books, reports, podcasts, and websites. For now, here are a few of our favourite go-to resources:

PART 1 The Purposeful Investor

- Alexander, Jon. *Citizens: When we start to think and act like citizens, not consumers, everything changes.* Kingston upon Thames (UK): Canbury Press, 2023.
- Anderson, Chris. *Infectious Generosity: The Ultimate Idea Worth Spreading.* New York: Crown, 2024
- Harding, Kelli. *The Rabbit Effect: Live Longer, Healthier, and Happier with the Groundbreaking Science of Kindness.* New York: Atria Books, 2019.
- Reasons to be Cheerful: Tonic for tumultuous times: https://reasonstobecheerful.world/

PART 2 The Purposeful Investment Landscape

Exploring the Landscape

- *Our money can change everything*, ShareAction: https://shareaction.org/resources-learning/savers-resource-hub

Traditional Wealth Management

- Dunn, Elizabeth and Michael Norton. *Happy Money: The Science of Happier Spending*. New York: Simon & Schuster, 2013.
- *Is your pension fuelling the climate crisis?*, Make My Money Matter: https://makemymoneymatter.co.uk/pensions/
- S&P Global, *All Things Sustainable* Podcast: https://www.spglobal.com/sustainable1/en/podcasts
- *The Good Lists*, Good With Money: https://good-with-money.com/category/good-lists/

Impact Investment

- Emerson, Jed (edi.). *The ImpactAssets Handbook for Investors: Generating Social and Environmental Value through Capital Investing*, London: Anthem Press, 2017.
- *Introduction to Impact Investing*, Impact Investing Institute: https://www.impactinvest.org.uk/learning-hub/introduction-to-impact-investing/#8

Philanthropic Giving

- Davies, Rhodri. *Philanthropisms*: https://whyphilanthropymatters.com/podcasts/

- Pallotta, Dan. *The Everyday Philanthropist: A Better Way to Make a Better World.* Hoboken (NJ): John Wiley & Sons, 2023.

Questions to Ask

- *The golden rules of investing*, Financial Conduct Authority: https://www.fca.org.uk/investsmart/golden-rules-investing

PART 3: Capital in Action

- Figueres, Christiana and Tom Rivett-Carnac. *The Future We Choose: Surviving the Climate Crisis.* New York: Alfred A. Knopf, 2020.
- Figueres, Christian, Tom Rivett-Carnac, Paul Dickinson. *Outrage + Optimism Podcast*:

  https://www.outrageandoptimism.org/
- *Self-help for Smart People*, Dan Harris 10% Happier: https://www.danharris.com/

Printed in Dunstable, United Kingdom

73061848R00109